Korean War

How an Outnumbered American Regiment Defeated the Chinese

(A Novel Based on the Courage and Sacrifice of a Real Three-war Marine)

Robert Wood

Published By **Percy Clint**

Robert Wood

All Rights Reserved

Korean War: How an Outnumbered American Regiment Defeated the Chinese (A Novel Based on the Courage and Sacrifice of a Real Three-war Marine)

ISBN 978-1-7781779-4-1

No part of this guidebook shall be reproduced in any form without permission in writing from the publisher except in the case of brief quotations embodied in critical articles or reviews.

Legal & Disclaimer

The information contained in this book is not designed to replace or take the place of any form of medicine or professional medical advice. The information in this book has been provided for educational & entertainment purposes only.

The information contained in this book has been compiled from sources deemed reliable, and it is accurate to the best of the Author's knowledge; however, the Author cannot guarantee its accuracy and validity and cannot be held liable for any errors or omissions. Changes are periodically made to this book. You must consult your doctor or get professional medical advice before using any of the suggested remedies, techniques, or information in this book.

Upon using the information contained in this book, you agree to hold harmless the Author from and against any damages, costs, and expenses, including any legal fees potentially resulting from the application of any of the information provided by this guide. This disclaimer applies to any damages or injury caused by the use and application, whether directly or indirectly, of any advice or information presented, whether for breach of contract, tort, negligence, personal injury, criminal intent, or under any other cause of action.

You agree to accept all risks of using the information presented inside this book. You need to consult a professional medical practitioner in order to ensure you are both able and healthy enough to participate in this program.

Table Of Contents

Chapter 1: Cause and Effects of Korean Way 1

Chapter 2: The North Korean Invasion 15

Chapter 3: North Korea To The Parallel .. 34

Chapter 4: The New War 54

Chapter 5: The Aftermath Of The War .. 100

Chapter 6: The Divided Peninsula Goes To War 106

Chapter 7: North Korea At The Rebound 116

Chapter 8: Regroup And Rethink 124

Chapter 9: The Art Of Ignoring War 137

Chapter 10: Aftermath Of The Armistice 144

Chapter 11: Current Relations Between North 153

Chapter 12: Japanese Control Of Korea 158

Chapter 13: General Douglas Macarthur 170

Chapter 14: The Third Battle Of Seoul ..182

Chapter 1: Cause And Effects Of Korean Way

The Korean War took place between the time period of June 25, 1950 and July 17, 1953. The two Korean regimes fighting against each were the Republic of Korean supported by the United Nations and the Democratic People's Republic of Korea and its allies.

Korea was an independent nation since the 7th century. However, certain parts of the country came under the Japanese jurisdiction as a consequence of the war that took place between China and Japan during the years 1894 to 1895.

Korea was engulfed completely by the Japanese forces in August 1910. With the culmination of the Second World War, Korea was taken over by United States and Soviet Union in unison. The US authorities sought help from the United Nations to end the issue of a conjugated occupation of Korea.

To resolve the conflict, the United Nations suggested elections in the country, which were drastically opposed by the communists in North and South Korea. While the United Stated desired to prevent the multiplication of communism; the Soviet Union wanted to extend it as far as possible throughout the world.

With Kim II-Sung at the helm of affairs in North Korea supported by the Soviet Union, forces under him attacked South Korea under the anti-communist government of Syngman Rhee on June 25, 1950.

China plunged into the war in order to gain mileage against the probability of a US invasion. The war ended on July 27, 1953 due to armistice. However, this was a momentary cease fire without the signing of any long term peace treaties.

One of the most obvious effects of the war as in the case of any conflict was high numbers of casualties. The Korean War widened the gap between the United States and the Soviet Union on the issue of communism.

The war also propagated animosity between the US and China. As a direct consequence of the fear of the repercussions of communism, the US arbitrated into Vietnam to abolish the possibility of another North Korea. South Korea became a permanent location for the American military troops.

Despite the armistice, the actual war has not ceased since then. Korea remains bifurcated with the two sides on constant war readiness. The economic wide between the two sides has also deepened with the passage of time.

While South Korea has progressed economically and technologically; North Korea remains as a poor and immensely militarized country. The nuclear tests and numerous missile tests conducted by North Korea pose a threat to South Korea as well as Japan.

The eight point peace agreement signed by the leaders of the two sides of Korea on October 4, 2007 did open avenues of talks, peace, economic cooperation, renewal of highway, air travel and train services. However, the unification of North and South Korea still remains a dream in the hearts of many.

THE DECISION FOR WAR

The Western bloc was surprised by North Korea's decision to invade South Korea. American intelligence reports had documented the DPRK's military buildup, and by June 1950 the CIA had concluded that the DPRK could invade South Korea.

Analysis of these reports by American civilian and military intelligence agencies was colored by the greater attention given to other areas of the world, previous false alarms of impending invasion, North Korean security measures, and the judgment that the DPRK was a firmly controlled satellite of the Soviet Union.

This interpretation held that the DPRK could not destroy the Republic of Korea (ROK) government without Soviet assistance and that the Soviets would not provide such assistance, fearing it would spark a general war with the United States.

Instead, American intelligence judged that the DPRK would continue its efforts to destabilize the ROK, a conclusion reinforced by the National Assembly elections in May 1950 that highlighted widespread dissatisfaction with the Rhee government in South Korea.

The DPRK, while dependent on Soviet military and economic aid, was not a client state completely controlled by the Soviet Union; the initiative for the invasion came from Kim Il Sung, who was committed to unifying the country under his rule. Kim petitioned Stalin several times in 1949 for permission to invade South Korea.

In late January 1950 Stalin finally gave his assent and dispatched large amounts of military aid and Soviet advisers to prepare the invasion.

Stalin finally approved Kim's request because the United States had withdrawn its last ground combat unit from South Korea in June 1949 and Kim promised that the Korean People's Army (KPA) could conquer the South before the United States could intervene decisively.

Another consideration was that the United States had indicated that Korea was not needed for "strategic purposes," a euphemism for bases from which to fight the Soviet Union in World War III. The chances of a direct confrontation with the United States thus appeared small.

Kim in June 1950 had good reason to be confident of a quick victory. A force of 135,000, about half of whom were veterans of the Soviet Army or the Chinese People's Liberation Army, the KPA had 8 full divisions, each including a regiment of artillery; 2 divisions at half strength; 2 separate regiments; an armored brigade with 120 Soviet T–34/85 medium tanks; and 5 border constabulary brigades.

In support of the KPA were 180 Soviet aircraft, mostly fighters and attack bombers, and a few naval patrol craft. Soviet advisers prepared an invasion plan that called for tank-led combined-arms forces to advance 15–20 kilometers per day, occupying Seoul within three days and completing the operation in 22–27 days. Stalin, however, would not permit the Soviet advisers to accompany the KPA once it crossed into South Korea.

The ROK Army of 95,000 men was far less fit for war. Raised as a constabulary during the

American occupation and assisted by the U.S. Military Advisory Group to the Republic of Korea (KMAG), the ROK Army had since April 1948 been fighting a bitter war against guerrillas who received support from the DPRK.

In 1948 and 1949 the ROK Army also fought battles in up to regimental strength with North Korean border constabulary units, with each side making incursions into the other's territory.

These operations had interfered with effective training for conventional operations, and in June 1950 three of the eight ROK divisions were dispersed for counterguerrilla duties or small-unit training.

The ROK Army was a light infantry force: its artillery totaled eighty-nine light 105-mm. howitzers outranged by KPA artillery, and it had neither tanks nor any antitank weapons effective against the T–34/85s.

The ROK Navy matched its North Korean counterpart, but the ROK Air Force had only a few trainers and liaison aircraft. U.S. equipment, war-worn when furnished to South Korean forces, had deteriorated further, and supplies on hand could sustain combat operations no longer than fifteen days.

The North Korean main attack was on the western side of the peninsula; the KPAquickly crushed South Korean defenses at the 38th Parallel and entered Seoul on June 28. (See Map 9.) A secondary attack down the peninsula's center encountered stiff resistance in rugged AMERICAN rain; the KPA had more success on the east coast in keeping pace with the main drive.

ROK units in the Seoul area withdrew in disorder and abandoned most of their equipment because the bridges over the Han River at the south edge of the city were prematurely demolished. North Korean units in the west halted briefly after capturing Seoul to bring tanks and artillery across the Han River.

In Washington, a fourteen-hour time difference made it June 24 when the North Koreans crossed the parallel, and the first report of the invasion arrived that night. The next day, at a meeting the United States requested, the UN Security Council adopted a resolution demanding an immediate cessation of hostilities and a withdrawal of North Korean forces to the 38th Parallel.

The USSR did not exercise its veto power against the resolution because the Soviet delegate had been boycotting the council since January 1950 in protest of the United Nation's decision not to recognize the People's Republic of China (PRC), recently victorious in the Chinese Civil War, as China's legitimate government.

On the night of the twenty-fifth, after meetings between officials of the State and Defense Departments and then between

President Harry S. Truman and his key advisers, the President directed General of the Army Douglas MacArthur, Commander in Chief of Far East Command (FEC), to supply ROK forces with ammunition and equipment, evacuate American dependents from Korea, and survey conditions on the peninsula to determine how best to further assist the republic.

The President also ordered the U.S. Seventh Fleet from its current location in Philippine and Ryukyu waters to Japan. On the twenty-sixth, in a broad interpretation of a UN Security Council request for "every assistance" in supporting the June 25 resolution, President Truman authorized General MacArthur to use air and naval strength against North Korean targets below the 38th Parallel.

The President also redirected the bulk of the Seventh Fleet to Taiwan; by standing between the Chinese Communists on the mainland and the Nationalists on the island it could discourage either one from attacking the other and thus prevent a widening of hostilities.

When it became clear in Washington on June 27 that North Korea would ignore the UN demands, the Security Council, again at the urging of the United States, asked member states to furnish military assistance to help South Korea repel the invasion.

President Truman immediately broadened the range of U.S. air and naval operations to include North Korea and authorized the use of U.S. Army troops to protect Pusan, Korea's major port at the southeastern tip of the peninsula.

MacArthur meanwhile had flown to Korea and, after witnessing failing ROK Army efforts in defenses south of the Han River, recommended to Washington that a U.S. Army regimental combat team (RCT) be committed immediately to support the ROK Army in the area south of Seoul.

He also proposed building up the American presence in Korea to a two-division force for a counteroffensive. President Truman on June 30 approved MacArthur's request to dispatch an RCT and then later that same day directed him to use all forces available to him.

Thus the United Nations for the first time since its founding reacted to aggression with a decision to use armed force. The United States would accept the largest share of the obligation in Korea but, still deeply tired of war, would do so reluctantly. President Truman later described his decision to enter the war as the hardest of his days in office.

A Communist Korea would pose a major threat to Japan and thus the U.S. position in Asia. Also, American leaders believed that the Soviets had ordered the DPRK to attack to test the Western bloc's resolve.

They feared that if South Korea fell, the USSR would be encouraged to attack other countries in this manner and other countries would doubt America's commitment to defend them from Communist aggression.

The American people, conditioned by World War II to battle on a grand scale to complete victory, would experience a deepening frustration over the Korean conflict, brought on in the beginning by embarrassing reversals on the battlefield.

Chapter 2: The North Korean Invasion

The North Korean invasion of South Korea on June 25, 1950, in a narrow sense was only an escalation of a continuing civil war among Koreans that began with Japan's defeat in 1945.

In a larger sense, the invasion marked the eruption of the Cold War between the United States and the USSR into open hostilities because each of the Great Powers backed one of the competing Korean governments.

The war that followed would devastate Korea, lead to a large expansion of the U.S. armed forces and America's military presence around the world, and frustrate many on both sides by ending in an armistice that left the peninsula still divided.

The Great Powers' connection to Korea dated back to the decision in August 1945 by the United States and the USSR to dismantle the Japanese colonial system there by dividing the peninsula into two occupation zones.

In December 1945 the United States and the USSR agreed to form a joint commission from among American and Soviet personnel in Korea that would recommend, after consultation with various Korean groups, the form of a government for Korea.

Almost all Koreans in 1945 desired an independent Korea, but there were many competing visions of how to organize a new government. Between September 1945 and August 1948, the United States became entangled in this complex and violent Korean struggle that occurred in the context of increasing tensions between the United States and the USSR.

Many Korean political groups in 1945 had Socialist or Leftist orientations or were openly Communist. Americans, both in the occupation force and in Washington, feared that these groups would create a Korea unfriendly to American interests, a fear intensified by reports coming out of the northern occupation zone that the Soviets were sponsoring a Communist revolution there led by Kim Il Sung.

By the summer of 1947 Kim Il Sung had crushed opposition to his rule in the north. In the south, violence had destroyed the political center and driven the Leftists and Communists underground or into the hills to begin preparations for a guerrilla war against the Rightist groups that the U.S. military government had favored.

Soviet intransigence in negotiations over Korea's future and the political violence in the South, which had erupted into rebellion against the Syngman Rhee regime in April 1948, led the United States to propose a United Nations Temporary Commission on Korea and an end to the American occupation of South Korea.

The United Nations accepted the proposal to supervise efforts to create a unified Korea through a national election; but Kim Il Sung refused to cooperate, and thus the elections for a new Korean legislature in May 1948 took place only in the U.S. zone.

Dominated by Rightist parties, the new legislature elected Rhee president of the republic in July 1948; on August 15 he was inaugurated, bringing an end to the U.S. occupation in southern Korea but not to the guerrilla war in the south.

In the north, the Soviets had withdrawn all but advisers and the Democratic People's Republic of Korea (DPRK), headed by Kim, was established in September 1948.

THE SOUTH TO THE NAKTONG

Ground forces available to MacArthur included the 1st Cavalry Division and the 7th, 24th, and 25th Infantry Divisions, all under the Eighth U.S. Army in Japan, and the 29th Regimental Combat Team on Okinawa.

While MacArthur in 1949 had relieved Eighth Army of most occupation duties in order to concentrate on combat training, the postwar economies had left its units inadequately prepared for battle.

The divisions' maneuverability and firepower were sharply reduced by a shortage of organic units, by a general understrength among existing units, and by the worn condition of weapons and equipment. Some weapons and ammunition, medium tanks and antitank ammunition in particular, could scarcely be found in the Far East.

MacArthur's air arm, the Far East Air Forces (FEAF), was organized principally for air defense; much of its strength consisted of short-range jet interceptors that had to fly from bases in Japan.

Propeller-driven F–51s stored in Japan and more of these World War II planes rushed from the United States would prove crucial in meeting close air support needs during the war's early months, because they could fly many sorties each day from Korean airfields.

Naval Forces Far East, MacArthur's sea arm, controlled only five combat ships and a skeleton amphibious force, although reinforcement was near in the Seventh Fleet.

When MacArthur received permission to commit ground units, the main North Korean force already had crossed the Han River. By July 3 a westward enemy attack had captured a major airfield at Kimpo and the West Sea port of Inch'on. Troops attacking south moved into the town of Suwon, twenty-five miles below Seoul, on the fourth.

During July MacArthur and Lt. Gen. Walton H. Walker, Eighth Army's commander, disregarded the principle of mass and committed units piecemeal to trade space for time as the speed of the North Korean drive threatened to outpace the Far East Command's ability to deploy American units from Japan.

Where to open a delaying action was clear, for there were few good roads in the profusion of mountains making up the Korean peninsula. The best of these below Seoul, running on a gentle diagonal line through Suwon, Osan, Taejon, and Taegu to the port of Pusan in the southeast, was the obvious main axis of North Korean advance.

Which unit to use was also clear: the 24th Infantry Division was stationed nearest the ports in southern Japan. On July 1 General Walker directed Maj. Gen. William F. Dean, the 24th's commander, to move immediately by air two rifle companies, reinforced with heavy mortars and recoilless rifles, to Korea, with the remainder of his division to follow as fast as available air and sea transport could move it.

The two reinforced companies, joined by a field artillery battery that had moved by sea, moved into positions astride the main road near Osan, ten miles below Suwon, by dawn on July 5.

Some Americans believed that the arrival of this 540-man force on the battlefield designated Task Force SMITH for its commander, Lt. Col. Charles B. Smith—from the Army that had defeated far stronger opponents five years earlier would so awe the KPA that it would withdraw.

Around 8:00 A.M. on a rainy July 5, a North Korean division supported by tanks attacked the Americans. Task Force SMITH lacked antitank mines, the fire of its recoilless rifles and 2.36-inch rocket launchers failed to penetrate the T–34 armor, and the artillery batteryquickly fired its six antitank rounds.

The North Korean tanks did not stop to support an infantry assault; the task force inflicted numerous casualties on the KPA infantry, but it was too small to prevent a North Korean double envelopment.

After Colonel Smith ordered a withdrawal, discipline broke down and the task force fell back in disarray with over 180 casualties and the loss of all equipment save small arms.

Another casualty was American morale as word of the defeat reached other units of the 24th Infantry Division then moving into delaying positions below Osan.

The next three delaying actions by the 24th Infantry Division had similar results. In each case a North Korean force used armor and infantry assaults against the front of the American position, accompanied by an infantry double envelopment that established roadblocks behind the

WILLIAM F. DEAN (1899–1981)

Commander of an infantry division in World War II, Dean served as the last military governor of South Korea in 1947–1948 and took command of the 24th Infantry Division in 1949.

On July 20, when a much larger North Korean tank-infantry force overran elements of the division at Taejon, Dean took to the streets to hunt tanks and then led a group of soldiers out of the town.

Becoming separated from the group, he evaded capture until August 25. Dean successfully resisted all attempts to force him to make statements that supported the enemy and was released in September 1953. For his actions in Taejon, Dean received the Medal of Honor.

American position. This tactic often resulted in American units' withdrawing in disarray, with the loss of weapons and equipment, to the next delaying position.

The heavy losses and relative ease with which the KPA broke through American positions, together with the physical strain of delay operations in the Korean summer and the poor performance of a number of unit commanders, sapped American morale.

By July 15 the 24th Infantry Division had been forced back sixty miles to Taejon, where it initially took position along the Kum River above the town. South Korean units, some just remnants and others still in good order, also fell back on either flank of the 24th.

Fifty-three UN members meanwhile signified support of the Security Council's June 27 action, and twenty-nine of these made specific offers of assistance. Ground, air, and naval forces eventually sent to assist South Korea would represent twenty UN members and one nonmember nation.

The United States, Great Britain, Australia, New Zealand, Canada, Turkey, Greece,

France, Belgium, Luxembourg, the Netherlands, Thailand, the Philippines, Colombia, and Ethiopia would furnish ground combat troops. India, Sweden, Norway, Denmark, and Italy (the non–United Nations country) would furnish medical units.

Air forces would arrive from the United States, Australia, and the Union of South Africa; naval forces would come from the United States, Great Britain, Australia, Canada, and New Zealand.

The wide response to the council's call pointed out the need for a unified command. Acknowledging the United States as the major contributor, the UN Security Council on July 7 asked it to form a command into which all forces would be integrated and to appoint a commander. In the evolving command structure, President Truman became executive agent for the UN Security Council.

The National Security Council, Department of State, and Joint Chiefs of Staff participated in developing the grand concepts of operations in Korea. In the strictly military channel, the Joint Chiefs issued instructions through the Army member to the unified command in the field, designated the United Nations Command (UNC) under the command of General MacArthur.

MacArthur superimposed the headquarters of his new command over that of his existing Far East Command. Air and naval units from other countries joined the Far East Air Forces and Naval Forces Far East, respectively.

MacArthur assigned command of ground troops in Korea to the Eighth Army, and General Walker established his headquarters at Taegu on July 15, assuming command of all American ground troops on the peninsula and, at the request of President Rhee, of the ROK Army. When ground forces from other nations reached Korea, they too were assigned to Eighth Army.

Between July 14 and 18, MacArthur moved the 25th Infantry and 1st Cavalry Divisions to Korea after cannibalizing the 7th Infantry Division to strengthen them. By then the battle for Taejon had opened. New 3.5-inch rocket launchers hurriedly airlifted from the United States proved effective against T–34 tanks, but three worn-out infantry battalions and the remnants of the 24th Infantry Division's 105-mm.

Howitzer battalions could not delay for long after two KPA divisions established bridgeheads over the Kum River and encircled the town. The 24th withdrew from Taejon and was relieved by the 1st Cavalry Division. In eighteen days the 24th had disrupted the timetable of the KPA's main attack but at the cost of over 30 percent of its men and most of its equipment.

After taking Taejon, the main North Korean force split, one division moving south to the coast then turning east along the lower coastline. The remainder of the force continued southeast beyond Taejon toward Taegu. Southward advances by the secondary attack forces in the central and eastern sectors matched the main thrust, all clearly aimed to converge on Pusan.

North Korean supply lines grew long in the advance and less and less tenable under heavy UNC air attacks, as FEAFquickly achieved air superiority and UNC warships wiped out North Korean naval opposition and clamped a tight blockade on the Korean coast.

These achievements and the arrival of two battalions of the 29th RCT from Okinawa notwithstanding, American and South Korean troops steadily gave way. American casualties now passed 6,000, and South Korean losses had reached 70,000.

Having run out of space to trade for time, Walker at the end of July ordered a stand along a 140-mile line arching from the Korean Strait to the Sea of Japan west and north of Pusan. His three understrength U.S. divisions occupied the western arc, basing their position on the Naktong River.

South Korean forces, which KMAG advisers had reorganized into five divisions, defended the northern segment. A long line and few troops kept positions thin in this Pusan Perimeter. But replacements and additional units now entering or on the way to Korea would help relieve the problem, and fair interior lines of communications radiating from Pusan allowed Walker to move troops and supplies with facility.

A motorized combined-arms force, the KPA had followed the few good roads south from the 38th Parallel; the delaying actions that ROK and American units fought along these roads during July, while dispiriting for the defenders in their immediate results, had robbed Kim Il Sung of his expected quick victory.

These actions had also cost the KPA some 58,000 trained men and many tanks. Raising brigades to division status and conscripting large numbers of recruits (many from overrun regions of South Korea), the KPA over the next month and a half committed thirteen infantry divisions and an armored division against Walker's perimeter.

But the additional strength failed to compensate for the loss of trained men and tanks suffered in the advance to the Naktong.

While air strikes against KPA supply lines significantly reduced the combat power it could mass against the UN perimeter, Eighth Army's defense hinged on a shuttling of scarce reserves to block a gap, reinforce a position, or counterattack wherever the threat appeared greatest at a given moment.

The North Koreans shifted their main attack to various points of the perimeter, seeking a decisive breakthrough, but General Walker made effective use of intelligence provided by intercepts of KPA communications to prevent serious enemy penetrations and inflict telling losses that steadily drew off North Korean offensive power. His own strength, meanwhile, was on the rise.

By mid-September he had over 500 medium tanks. Replacements, many of them recalled Army reservists, arrived. Additional units came in: the 5th Regimental Combat Team from Hawaii, the 2d Infantry Division and 1st Provisional Marine Brigade from the United States, and a two-battalion British infantry brigade from Hong Kong.

For the 1st Cavalry and 24th and 25th Infantry Divisions, infantry battalions and artillery batteries hastily assembled in the United States arrived to bring these divisions to their full complement of subordinate units. Bomber and fighter squadrons also arrived to strengthen the FEAF.

Thus, as the U.S. Army advisers had worked with the ROK Army since its organization in 1946 as the Korean National Constabulary. With the withdrawal of U.S. forces from Korea in 1949, KMAG was activated to continue this work. KMAG used the counterpart system, pairing American officers with Korean commanders down to the battalion level and with key staff officers.

During the war, much of KMAG's effort necessarily went into providing advisers for units in combat; but it also supervised the training of the many new units the ROK Army organized.

Chapter 3: North Korea To The Parallel

General MacArthur at the entry of U.S. forces into Korea had perceived that the deeper the North Koreans drove, the more vulnerable they would become to a turning movement delivered by an amphibious assault.

He began work on plans for such a blow almost at the start of hostilities, favoring Inch'on, the West Sea port halfway up the west coast, as the landing site. Just twenty-five miles east lay Seoul, where Korea's main roads and rail lines converged.

A force landing at Inch'on would have to move inland only a short distance to cut North Korean supply routes, and the recapture of the capital city could also have a helpful psychological impact.

Combined with a general northward advance by the Eighth Army, a landing at Inch'on could produce decisive results. Enemy troops retiring before the Eighth

Army would be cut off by the amphibious force behind them or be forced to make a slow and difficult withdrawal through the mountains farther east.

Though pressed to meet Eighth Army troop requirements, MacArthur was able to shape a two-division landing force. He formed the headquarters of the X Corps from members of his own staff, naming his chief of staff, Maj. Gen. Edward M. Almond, as corps commander.

He rebuilt the 7th Infantry Division by giving it high priority on replacements from the United States and by assigning it 8,600 South Korean recruits, most of them poorly trained. The latter measure was part of a larger program, the Korean Augmentation to the United States Army (KATUSA). The KATUSA program began when the U.S.

Army could not supply Eighth Army with all the replacements it required. KATUSAs, usually newly conscripted South Koreans, were assigned mostly to American infantry units.

At the same time Almond acquired from the United States the greater part of the 1st Marine Division, which he planned to fill out with the Marine brigade currently in the Pusan Perimeter. The X Corps, with these two divisions, the ROK 17th Infantry, and two ROK Marine Corps battalions, was to make its landing as a separate force, not as part of the Eighth Army.

Many judged the Inch'on plan dangerous. Naval officers considered the extreme Yellow Sea tides and narrow channel approaches to Inch'on, easily blocked by mines, as big risks to shipping. Marine officers saw danger in landing in the middle of a built-up area and in having to scale high sea walls to get ashore.

The Joint Chiefs of Staff (JCS) anticipated serious consequences if the Inch'on plan failed, since MacArthur would be committing his last major units.

The General Reserve in the United States was nearly exhausted by September 1: the 187th Airborne RCT and the 3d Infantry Division would arrive in Japan in mid-September, but the 3d would need time to recover after being stripped to provide men for Eighth Army, leaving the 82d Airborne

Division the only uncommitted major unit. The Army had begun a substantial expansion, activating new Regular units and mobilizing National Guard and Organized Reserve Corps units; but this increase would not yield combat ready units until 1951. In light of the uncertainties, MacArthur's decision was a remarkable gamble; but if results are what count, his action was one of exemplary boldness.

The 1st Marine Division swept into Inch'on on September 15 against light resistance. Although opposition stiffened, X Corps steadily pushed inland over the next two weeks.

One arm struck south and seized Suwon, while the remainder of the corps cleared Kimpo Airfield, crossed the Han, and fought through Seoul. MacArthur, with dramatic ceremony, returned the capital city to President Rhee on September 29.

General Walker meanwhile attacked out of the Pusan Perimeter on September 16. His forces gained ground slowly at first; but on September 23, after the portent of Almond's envelopment and Walker's frontal attack became clear, the North Korean forces broke.

The Eighth Army, by then organized as 4 corps, 2 U.S. and 2 ROK, rolled forward in pursuit, linking with the X Corps on September 26. About 30,000 North Korean troops escaped above the 38th Parallel through the eastern mountains.

Several thousand more bypassed in the pursuit hid in the mountains of South Korea to fight as guerrillas. But by the end of September the Korean People's Army ceased to exist as an organized force anywhere in the Southern republic.

NOTH KOREA TO THE YALU

In 1950 President Truman frequently described the American-led effort in Korea as a police action, a euphemism for the war that produced both criticism and amusement. But the President's term was an honest reach for perspective.

Determined to halt the aggression, he was equally determined to limit hostilities to the peninsula and to avoid taking steps that would prompt Soviet or Chinese participation.

By Western estimates, Europe with its highly developed industrial resources, not Asia, held the high place on the Communist schedule of expansion; hence, the North

Atlantic Treaty Organization (NATO) alliance needed the deterrent strength that otherwise would be drawn off by a heavier involvement in the Far East.

Indeed, Truman and many of his advisers, believing that Kim Il Sung was Stalin's puppet, suspected that Stalin had ordered the DPRK to attack in order to weaken the West's defenses elsewhere.

To counter that possibility and to reassure America's allies, Truman in July had ordered a massive expansion of the U.S. armed forces, an enormous increase in nuclear weapons production, and a great increase in military aid to other nations.

To reinforce NATO, the President in September announced a major buildup of American forces in Europe. For the Army, this meant dispatching four divisions and other units to Germany during 1951, where they joined the 1st Infantry Division to form the Seventh Army.

On this and other bases, a case could be made for halting Mac-Arthur's forces at the 38th Parallel. In reestablishing the old border, the UNC had met the UN call for assistance in repelling the attack on South Korea.

In an early statement, Secretary of State Dean Acheson had said the United Nations was intervening "solely for the purpose of restoring the Republic of Korea to its status prior to the invasion from the north." A halt, furthermore, would be consistent with the U.S. policy of containment.

There were, on the other hand, substantial military reasons to carry the war into North Korea. Failure to destroy the 30,000 North Korean troops who had escaped above the parallel and an estimated 30,000 more in northern training camps could leave South Korea in little better position than before the start of hostilities.

Complete military victory, by all appearances within easy grasp, also would achieve the longstanding U.S. and UN objective of reunifying Korea.

Against these incentives had to be balanced muted warnings against a UNC entry into North Korea from both Communist China and the USSR in August and September. But these were counted as attempts to discourage the UNC, not as genuine threats to enter the war. President Truman decided to order the Eighth Army into North Korea.

On September 27, the JCS sent MacArthur instructions for future operations. The directive authorized him to cross the 38th Parallel in pursuit of his military objective, the destruction of the North Korean armed forces. Once he had achieved that objective, he was to occupy North Korea and await action by the United Nations on the unification of Korea.

To avoid escalation of the conflict, MacArthur could not enter North Korea if major Chinese or Soviet forces entered North Korea before his forces did or if the USSR or the PRC announced it intended to enter.

As a further safeguard, MacArthur was to use only Korean forces in the extreme northern territory abutting the Yalu River boundary with Manchuria and that in the far northeast along the Tumen River boundary with the USSR.

Ten days later the UN General Assembly voted for the restoration of peace and security throughout Korea, thereby approving the UNC's entry into North Korea.

There were two options for the invasion of North Korea. General MacArthur considered the best option keeping the X Corps separate from the Eighth Army and withdrawing it through Inch'on and Pusan to conduct an amphibious assault at

Wonsan, North Korea's major seaport on the east coast, while the Eighth Army advanced on P'yongyang, the DPRK's capital. Both forces would then move to the Yalu.

This option reflected MacArthur's conclusion that an amphibious attack on Wonsan would allow the X Corps to operate without burdening the Eighth Army's logistical system and would trap thousands of retreating KPA troops and that he could coordinate both forces from Japan.

Another factor was that MacArthur had been favorably impressed by General Almond's performance. General Walker, who did not have as close a relationship with Mac-Arthur as did General Almond, considered the best option the assignment of the X Corps to the Eighth Army.

The X Corps already was in position to continue the attack toward P'yongyang, and other divisions could drive east across the peninsula to Wonsan, linking up with the ROK I Corps moving up the east coast. The Eighth Army would then advance north to the Yalu.

This option, Eighth Army planners concluded, made the best use of the limited UNC logistical capabilities and maintained the momentum of the UNC's advance, since the Eighth Army's I Corps would have to pause before advancing on P'yongang. Walker, however, never formally presented this option to MacArthur, and the October 2 UNC order to advance used MacArthur's concept.

President Rhee, impatient to unify his country, had already directed the ROK I Corps on the east coast to advance; it crossed the parallel on October 1 and captured Wonsan on the tenth. The ROK II Corps at nearly the same time opened an advance through central North Korea.

On October 7 the I Corps moved north, and on October 19 it entered P'yongyang. Five days later the corps had advanced to the Ch'ongch'on River within fifty miles of the Manchurian border. The ROK II Corps veered northwest to come alongside.

To the east, past the unoccupied spine of the axial Taebaek Mountains, the ROK I Corps by October 24 moved above Wonsan, entering Iwon on the coast and approaching the huge Changjin Reservoir.

Meanwhile, the X Corps had boarded ships at Pusan and Inch'on, in the process greatly impeding the flow of supplies to Eighth Army, and sailed for Wonsan. Although the ROK I Corps had captured the port earlier, the X Corps had to wait until October 26 to begin landing in order to allow UNC naval forces to clear the heavily mined coastal waters.

Despite this setback, the outlook for the UNC in the last week of October was distinctly optimistic. The KPA had collapsed as an effective military force. Despite further warnings emanating from Communist China, American civilian and military leaders concluded that Chinese intervention was very unlikely, and that if the PRC did dispatch units of the People's Liberation Army to Korea, UNC air power would destroy them.

After meeting with MacArthur at Wake Island on October 15, President Truman revised his instructions to MacArthur only to the extent that if Chinese forces should appear in Korea, MacArthur should continue his advance if he believed his forces had a reasonable chance of success.

In hopes of ending operations before the onset of winter, MacArthur on October 24 ordered his ground commanders to advance to the northern border as rapidly as possible and with all forces available. In the west, the Eighth Army sent several columns toward the Yalu, each free to advance as fast and/or as far as possible without regard for the progress of the others.

General Almond, adding the ROK I Corps to his command upon landing, proceeded to clear northeastern Korea. The ROK I Corps advanced up the coast, closing to within sixty-five miles of the Soviet border by November 21, while the 1st Marine and the 7th Infantry Divisions moved through the mountains toward the Yalu and the Changjin Reservoir.

In the United States, a leading newspaper expressed the prevailing optimism with the editorial comment that "Except for unexpected developments … we can now be easy in our minds as to the military outcome."

Unexpected developments soon occurred. Mao Zedong had decided to intervene and dispatched an expeditionary force, called the Chinese People's Volunteer Force (CPVF), across the Yalu. Highly skilled in camouflage, hundreds of Chinese units had moved into North Korea without detection.

In the Eighth Army zone, the first Chinese soldier was discovered among captives taken on October 25 by the I Corps' 1st ROK Division and units of the ROK II Corps. The Chinese attacked both of Eighth Army's corps, inflicting especially heavy losses on ROK units and on a regiment of the 1st Cavalry Division when it came forward at Unsan to cover the withdrawal of the 1st ROK Division.

General Walker ordered the I Corps and the ROK II Corps to fall back on the Ch'ongch'on River to regroup and ordered the IX Corps forward to the Ch'ongch'on. Once that corps had arrived, Walker planned to resume the advance in accordance with MacArthur's orders.

The Chinese forces continued to attack until November 6, when they abruptly broke contact. In the X Corps zone, the Chinese stopped a ROK column on the mountain road leading to the Changjin Reservoir.

American marines relieved the South Koreans and by November 6 pushed through the resistance to within a few miles of the reservoir, whereupon the Chinese also broke contact.

At first it appeared that individual Chinese soldiers, possibly volunteers, had reinforced the North Koreans. The estimate rose higher by November 24, but interrogation of captives did not convince Far East Command that there had been a large Chinese commitment.

Aerial observation of the Yalu and the ground below the river did not detect signs of such a commitment, and the voluntary withdrawal from contact on November 6 seemed no logical part of a full Chinese effort. (In fact, the Chinese withdrew because they had achieved their first objectives, forcing the UNC advance to pause and evaluating UNC units' performance.)

Some commanders, notably Generals Walker, Almond, and Paik Sun Yup, the 1st ROK Division commander, did believe that the Chinese had intervened in strength.

General MacArthur, however, concluded that the PRC would not mount a full-scale offensive. Confident that UNC air power and American artillery would destroy any Chinese expeditionary force, he ordered the advance to the Yalu resumed.

In northeastern Korea, the X Corps, now strengthened by the arrival of the 3d Infantry Division, resumed its advance on November 11. In the west, General Walker requested a delay until November 24; Eighth Army's supply lines were still inadequate, and he wanted the IX Corps to complete its move.

The Chinese were waiting to catch Eighth Army as it left its defensive positions along the Ch'ongch'on; on the night of November 25, one day after the Eighth Army resumed its advance, the Chinese launched a massive offensive to eject UNC forces from North Korea.

Strong CPVF attacks hit the Eighth Army's IX and ROK II Corps, collapsing the ROK II Corps on the army's right flank. On the twenty-seventh the attacks engulfed the leftmost forces of the X Corps at the Changjin Reservoir, and by the next day the UNC position in North Korea began to crumble.

"Except for unexpected developments ... we can now be easy in our minds as to the military outcome." "We face an entirely new war," MacArthur notified Washington on November 28.

On the following day he instructed General Walker to make whatever withdrawals were necessary to escape being enveloped by Chinese pushing hard and deep through the hole left by ROK II Corps' collapse and ordered the X Corps to pull into a beachhead around the east coast port of Hungnam, north of Wonsan.

The entirely new war also featured Soviet Mig–15 jet interceptors flown by Soviet pilots from bases in Manchuria protected by Soviet antiaircraft units. To counter this new threat, the U.S. Air Force hurriedly dispatched its premier jet fighter, the F–86, to Korea.

Stalin, fearing that the evidence provided by the body of a Soviet pilot would force the U.S. government to strike directly at the USSR, limited his air units to operations over Communist-controlled territory. The Soviets trained Chinese and Korean units in the Mig–15, but FEAF defeated attempts later in the war to stage these units in North Korea by bombing their airfields.

Chapter 4: The New War

Eighth Army's withdrawal from the Ch'ongch'on led to one of the greatest ordeals ever suffered by a U.S. division. Chinese forces established a strong roadblock below the town of

On November 25, 1950, General Almond ordered the 7th Infantry Division to move one RCT to the east side of the Changjin Reservoir to cover the advance of the 1st Marine Division to the Yalu.

Consisting of little more than two weak infantry battalions and an artillery battalion, this force was initially known as Task Force MACLEAN after its commander, Col. Allan D. MacLean.

When the Chinese attacked the X Corps on the night of November 27–28, the task force held on the east side of the reservoir for four days. On December 1 Lt. Col. Don C. Faith, Jr., who had taken command after the capture of Colonel MacLean, ordered a breakout to the south.

Low on ammunition, worn down by extreme cold and bitter fighting, and burdened with many wounded, the task force was stopped at a Chinese roadblock and destroyed. About 1,000 of the soldiers were killed, taken prisoner, or declared missing, including Colonel Faith, who received a posthumous Medal of Honor. Their ordeal was not in vain, and their sacrifice helped save the 1st Marine Division.

Convoy from Wonsan to Hamhung, Robert Weldy Baer, 1950 Kunu-ri and took positions on the hills along the road on which the 2d Infantry Division was moving. Already weakened by several days of combat in bitter cold weather, on November 30 most of the division literally had to run a gauntlet of fire that tore units apart.

Emerging from the gauntlet with about one-third of its men dead, wounded, or missing and most of its equipment lost, the division staggered back into South Korea to refit.

General Walker initially believed that he could hold a line based on P'yongyang, but he quickly concluded that the Chinese would be able to outflank such a line and pin down the Eighth Army.

This conclusion, as well as his concern that his still inadequate supply lines would negate Eighth Army's firepower advantage, led him to abandon P'yongyang and withdraw to positions north of Seoul.

There, he hoped, shorter supply lines, better defensive terrain, and the arrival of the X Corps from northeastern Korea would allow Eighth Army to repeat against the Chinese the strategy that had defeated the KPA. The light infantry Chinese force could not keep up with the motorized Eighth Army, and the latter withdrew into South Korea without opposition.

In the X Corps' withdrawal to Hungnam, the center and rightmost units experienced little difficulty. But the 1st Marine Division and the remnants of the 7th infantry Division task force at the Changjin Reservoir encountered Chinese positions overlooking the mountain road leading to the sea. Marine Maj. Gen. O. P. Smith skillfully led a withdrawal that reached the coast on December 11.

General MacArthur briefly visualized the X Corps beachhead at Hungnam as a "geographic threat" that could deter Chinese to the west from deepening their advance. Later, with prompting from the Joint Chiefs, he ordered the X Corps to withdraw by sea and proceed to Pusan, where it would join Eighth Army, ending its independent status.

Almond started the evacuation on the eleventh, contracting the Hungnam perimeter as he loaded troops and materiel aboard ships in the harbor. With little interference from enemy forces, which had suffered heavy casualties from American firepower and the extreme cold, he completed the evacuation and set sail for Pusan on Christmas Eve.

A highly regarded corps commander in World War II, Walker took command of Eighth Army in 1948 and supervised its shift from an occupation force to one focused on readiness. He skillfully used Eighth Army's slender reserves to counter breakthroughs on the Pusan Perimeter, frequently flying at low altitude to reconnoiter the front line.

The defeat in North Korea and the withdrawal into South Korea gravely damaged Eighth Army's morale, but Walker had little opportunity to reverse this damage before he died in a vehicle accident on December 23, 1950. He was promoted posthumously to the rank of four-star general.

The day before General Walker was killed in a motor vehicle accident while traveling north from Seoul toward the front. Lt. Gen. Matthew B. Ridgway flew from Washington to assume command of the Eighth Army.

After conferring in Tokyo with MacArthur, who instructed Ridgway to hold a position as far north as possible but in any case to maintain the Eighth Army intact, the new army commander reached Korea on the twenty-sixth.

Ridgway himself wanted at least to hold the Eighth Army in its positions north of Seoul and to attack if possible. But his initial inspection of the front raised serious doubts. Deeply unsatisfied with the caliber of Eighth Army's senior leadership, he began arrangements to remove those officers who failed to meet his standards.

The sudden reversal of fortune in combat, the long retreat without significant enemy contact, and the bitter winter weather for which most troops did not have the proper clothing and equipment had so worn down Eighth Army's morale that Ridgway judged it temporarily incapable of mounting effective large-scale offensive actions.

He also discovered much of the defense line to be thin and weak. The Chinese had finally caught up with Eighth Army and appeared to be massing in the west for a push on Seoul, and twelve reconstituted North Korean divisions seemed to be concentrating for an attack in the central region. From all available evidence, New Year's Day seemed a logical date for the enemy's opening assault.

To strengthen the line, Ridgway committed the 2d Infantry Division to the central sector where positions were weakest, even though that unit had not fully recovered from losses in the Kunu-ri gauntlet, and pressed General Almond toquicken the preparation of the X Corps whose forces needed refitting before moving to the front.

Realizing that time probably was against him, he also ordered his western units to organize a bridgehead above Seoul, one deep enough to protect the Han River bridges, from which to cover a withdrawal below the city should an enemy offensive compel a general retirement.

Enemy forces opened attacks on New Year's Eve, directing their major effort toward Seoul. When the offensive gained momentum, Ridgway ordered his western forces back to the Seoul bridgehead and pulled the Withdrawal from Kot'o-ri, 1950, Henrietta Snowden, 2000 rest of the Eighth Army to positions roughly on line to the east.

After strong Chinese units assaulted the bridgehead, he withdrew to a line forty miles below Seoul. In the west, the last troops pulled out of Seoul on January 4, 1951, demolishing the Han bridges on the way out as the Chinese entered the city from the north.

Only light Chinese forces pushed south of the city, and enemy attacks in the west diminished. In central and eastern Korea, North Korean forces pushed forward; but the 1st Marine Division cut off and then destroyed them.

This pause highlighted a major Communist operational weakness: the enemy's logistical system, short of mechanical transport and with lengthening supply lines under FEAF attack, permitted him to undertake offensive operations for no more than a week or two before he had to pause for replacements and supplies.

Ridgway used this pause to continue his rehabilitation of Eighth Army's aggressive spirit and to introduce a new operational concept. Gaining territory would be incidental to inflicting maximum casualties on the enemy at minimum cost to UNC units.

On the attack or on the defense, Ridgway insisted that his units always maintain contact with the enemy and use every available source of firepower—infantry, armor, artillery, and air—against them.

Ridgway expected that the tremendous losses these "meat grinder" tactics would inflict on Communist units would at least greatly assist the advance of the Eighth Army to the 38th Parallel and at best convince the enemy to end the war.

In mid-January the Eighth Army began RCT-size probes forward of UNC lines to gather intelligence and inflict losses on the enemy with meat grinder tactics. These probes, carefully planned to ensure success, had a further objective: to restore the Eighth Army's confidence and aggressiveness.

These operations met all their goals, and Ridgway grew confident that the Eighth Army would hold. On January 25 the I and IX

Corps began a slow advance forward by phase lines to prevent units from being cut.

A well-respected commander of an airborne division and a corps during World War II, General Ridgway in 1950 was the Army's Deputy Chief of Staff for Administration and played a key role in mobilizing the service for war. His success in reviving the Eighth Army in 1951 led to his selection to replace MacArthur as Commander in Chief of the Far East Command.

Promoted to four-star general in May 1951, Ridgway in 1952 succeeded Eisenhower as the Supreme Allied Commander in Europe. Eisenhower selected Ridgway in 1953 to be the Army's Chief of Staff, but the general strenuously argued against the President's New Look strategy. Because of this disagreement, Eisenhower did not reappoint him to a second term as Chief of Staff and Ridgway retired in 1955.

General Ridgway off, and on January 30 Ridgway ordered the rest of Eighth Army to advance in a similar manner.

Where Ridgway grew more confident, MacArthur was far less optimistic. Earlier, in acknowledging the Chinese intervention, he had notified Washington that the Chinese could drive the UNC out of Korea unless he received major reinforcement.

At the time, however, there were no major reinforcements available; the Army was still rebuilding the General Reserve and had ordered more National Guard and Reserve units mobilized, but these efforts could not produce ready units until mid-1951.

The massive military buildup begun earlier in 1950, in any case, had not been ordered with commitment in Korea in mind. The main concern in Washington was the possibility that the Chinese entry into Korea was only one part of a USSR move toward global war, a concern great enough to lead

President Truman to declare a state of national emergency on December 16.

Washington officials in any event considered Korea no place to become involved in a major war. For all these reasons, the Joint Chiefs of Staff notified MacArthur that a major buildup of UNC forces was out of the question. MacArthur was to stay in Korea if he could; but should the Chinese drive UNC forces back on Pusan, the Joint Chiefs would order a withdrawal to Japan.

Contrary to the reasoning in Washington, MacArthur meanwhile proposed four retaliatory measures against the Chinese: blockade the China coast, destroy China's war industries through naval and air attacks, reinforce the troops in Korea with Chinese Nationalist forces, and allow diversionary operations by Nationalist troops against the China mainland.

These proposals for escalation received serious study in Washington but were eventually discarded in favor of sustaining the policy that confined the fighting to Korea.

Interchanges between Washington and Tokyo next centered on the timing of a withdrawal from Korea. MacArthur believed that Washington should establish all the criteria of an evacuation, whereas Washington wanted MacArthur first to provide the military guidelines on timing.

The whole issue was finally settled after General J. Lawton Collins, Army Chief of Staff, visited Korea, saw that the Eighth Army was improving under Ridgway's leadership, and became as confident as Ridgway that the Chinese would be unable to drive the Eighth Army off the peninsula.

The Eighth Army continued its cautious northward advance in early February and retook Inch'on; but there were growing indications of Chinese preparations for another offensive in the center of the peninsula.

That offensive began on the night of February 11–12, and Chinese attacksquickly crushed the X Corps' ROK 8th Division and badly damaged two other ROK divisions in the corps.

Because ROK divisions had little artillery, X Corps had attached, via cumbersome command and control arrangements, U.S. artillery support forces to these divisions. The unwieldy arrangements prevented the 8th ROK Division support force's receiving timely permission to withdraw; most of this artillery force, taken from the 2d Infantry Division, was destroyed.

The X Corps fell back on the key road junction of Wonju. There, American and South Korean units applied Ridgway's new operational concept, shredding repeated Chinese attacks on the town.

On the X Corps western flank, the 2d Infantry Division's 23d RCT, with an attached French battalion, had dug in at Chip'yong-ni, another key road junction. Cut off from the rest of Eighth Army, the force defeated attacks by six CPVF regiments.

For Ridgway, the defeat of the Communists' February offensive showed that his operational concept was a success and, more importantly, that his army had recovered its spirit. He ordered the Eighth Army to continue the advance.

The Communists offered only light resistance as they withdrew, and on March 14 the I Corps liberated Seoul. Between March 27 and 31, the Eighth Army closed in on the 38th Parallel. From there, it advanced, again with little resistance to a line, designated KANSAS, which followed the Imjin River in the west and the east to the coast near Yangyang.

Most of the Eighth Army began digging in on Line KANSAS in preparation for the Chinese offensive expected sometime later in the spring. Ridgway sent elements of the I and IX Corps toward the Iron Triangle in central Korea.

This area, 20–30 miles above the 38th Parallel and bounded by P'yongyang in the north and Ch'orwon and Kumwha in the south, was in the gap between northern and southern ranges of the Taebaek Mountains and connected the eastern and western halves of the Communist front. Key road and rail links ran through this area, and it had become a vital logistical area for the CPVF and the KPA.

In Washington, President Truman and his military and civilian advisers had been considering the possibility that, with the Eighth Army's northward advance and the heavy casualties it had inflicted on the enemy, the Communists might be willing to open negotiations.

The United Nation's call to eject the invaders from South Korea had again been achieved; and both in Washington and in other capitals, there was growing sentiment that this achievement was sufficient and that unification of Korea should be negotiated after the war.

On March 20 the Joint Chiefs notified MacArthur that a presidential announcement was being drafted that would indicate a willingness to negotiate with the Chinese and the North Koreans to make "satisfactory arrangements for concluding the fighting." They asked for MacArthur's recommendations on what latitude he required for operating north of the 38th Parallel.

Before the President could make his announcement, MacArthur on March 24 issued his own offer to enemy commanders to discuss an end to the fighting, but it was an offer that placed the UNC in the role of victor and indeed sounded like an ultimatum.

"The enemy … must by now be painfully aware," MacArthur said in part, "that a decision of the United Nations to depart from its tolerant effort to contain the war to the area of Korea, through an expansion of our military operations to its coastal areas and interior bases, would doom Red China to the risk of imminent military collapse."

President Truman considered the statement at cross-purposes with the one he would have issued and so canceled his own, hoping the enemy might sue for an armistice if kept under pressure.

While President Truman after this episode considered relieving Mac- Arthur, he had yet to make a final decision when the next incident occurred. On April 5 Joseph W. Martin, Republican leader in the House of Representatives, rose and read MacArthur's response to a request for comment on an address Martin had made suggesting the use of Nationalist Chinese forces to open a second front.

In that response, MacArthur said he believed in "meeting force with maximum counterforce" and that the use of Nationalist Chinese forces fitted that belief. Convinced, also, that "if we lose this war to Communism in Asia the fall of Europe is inevitable, win it and Europe most probably would avoid war." He added that there could be "no substitute for victory" in Korea.

President Truman could not accept MacArthur's open disagreement with and effort to change national policy. Concluding that Mac-Arthur was "unable to give his wholehearted support to the policies of the United States government and of the United Nations in matters pertaining to his official duties," President Truman recalled MacArthur on April 11 and named General Ridgway his successor.

MacArthur returned to the United States to receive the acclaim of a nation shocked by the relief of one of its greatest military heroes. Before the Congress and the public, he defended his own views against those of the Truman administration. The controversy was to endure for many months, but in the end the nation accepted the fact that whatever the merit

MacArthur returned to the United States to receive the acclaim of a nation shocked by the relief of one of its greatest military heroes. Of MacArthur's arguments the President as Commander in Chief had cause to relieve him.

Lt. Gen. James A. Van Fleet, commander of the Second Army in the United States, was selected to succeed Ridgway as commander of the Eighth Army.

On April 14 General Ridgway turned over the Eighth Army to General Van Fleet and left for Tokyo to take up his new duties. The drive toward the Iron Triangle had continued during this time; however, there were increasing indications that the Communists were nearly ready to launch another offensive.

On April 22 twenty-one Chinese and nine North Korean divisions launched strong attacks in western and central Korea and lighter attacks in the east, with the major effort aimed against the I Corps defending the approaches to Seoul. The ROK 6th Division, on the IX Corps left flank, immediately collapsed, which threatened the I Corps with envelopment.

This threat and the sheer weight of the Chinese forces targeting Seoul forced the I and IX Corps to withdraw, in good order and inflicting severe casualties on the Chinese as they moved, through successive delaying positions to previously established defenses a few miles north of Seoul. There, the UNC's terrific firepower advantage and the weaknesses of the Chinese logistical system halted the enemy advance.

When enemy forces withdrew to reorganize, Van Fleet laid plans for a return to Line KANSAS but then postponed the countermove when his intelligence sources indicated he had stopped only the first effort of the enemy offensive.

Instead, he directed his senior commanders to fortify positions and prepare to fire artillery at up to five times the standard U.S. Army daily rate of fire, a measure that came to be called the Van Fleet Day of Fire.

The Communists renewed their offensive after darkness on May 15. Van Fleet had expected the major assault again to be directed against Seoul, but enemy forces this time drove hardest in the east.

One of the outstanding combat leaders of World War II, General Van Fleet in 1948–1950 headed the American advisory effort in Greece, transforming the Greek Army into an effective force that won the civil war there.

Following Eighth Army's victories in the spring of 1951, he several times proposed a major offensive into North Korea to bring the war to an end. Promoted to four-star general in July 1951, Van Fleet established a close relationship with the ROK Army and was instrumental in improving its performance.

After the apparent death of his son, an Air Force pilot declared missing in action over North Korea, Van Fleet relinquished command of Eighth Army in February 1953. After retiring the next month, Van Fleet sharply criticized the decision not to seek a decisive military victory.

Two of the X Corps' ROK divisionsquickly gave way under Chinese assaults, and KPA and CPVF attacks to the east of the X Corps shattered the ROK III Corps by May 18. While Van Fleet shifted units from the west, the X Corps' 2d Infantry Division bent its line back and denied the Chinese a decisive breakthrough.

Applications of the Van Fleet Day of Fire destroyed entire CPVF and KPA units, and by May 20 the Eighth Army had defeated the offensive. Determined to destroy the enemy's remaining major units, Van Fleet immediately ordered a counterattack.

These units, however, had already begun withdrawing; this head start, monsoon rains, and mountainous terrain prevented the Eighth Army from catching them. By May 31 the Eighth Army was just short of Line KANSAS.

The next day Van Fleet sent part of his force toward Line WYOMING, whose seizure would give him control of the lower portion of the Iron Triangle. The Eighth Army occupied both Line KANSAS and the WYOMING bulge by mid-June.

Since the KANSAS-WYOMING Line followed ground suitable for a strong defense, the Joint Chiefs directed that the Eighth Army hold that line and wait for a bid for armistice negotiations from the Chinese and North Koreans, who should have realized by this time that their committed forces lacked the ability to conquer South Korea.

In line with this decision, Van Fleet began to fortify his positions. Enemy forces meanwhile used the respite from attack to recoup heavy losses and to develop defenses opposite the Eighth Army. The fighting lapsed into patrolling and small local clashes.

The Static War

After back-channel coordination through George W. Kennan, a prominent American diplomat on leave from the State Department, Jacob Malik, the Soviet delegate to the United Nations, on June 23, 1951, announced in New York during a broadcast of a UN radio program that the USSR believed the war in Korea could be settled by negotiations.

"Discussions," he said, "should be started between the belligerents for a cease-fire and an armistice." When the PRC endorsed Malik's proposal over Beijing radio, President Truman authorized General Ridgway to arrange armistice talks with his enemy counterpart.

A company-size position established in 1952 as part of the UN outpost line, this outpost's nickname came from its shape on the map. Pork Chop became emblematic of the combat actions fought during the war's final eighteen months. The Chinese launched three major attacks in 1953 to take the outpost; and the third attack, starting on July 6, was the heaviest.

The 7th Infantry Division rotated five infantry battalions in five days through the position to hold it with the assistance of tremendous amounts of artillery fire.

With the Chinese apparently determined to take the outpost at whatever cost and an armistice imminent, General Taylor ordered Pork Chop Hill abandoned. Through a clever ruse, the 7th Infantry Division removed its troops during the day on July 11 without any casualties.

At the first armistice conference the two delegations agreed that hostilities would continue until an armistice agreement was signed. By July 26 the two delegations fixed the points to be settled in order to achieve an armistice.

But China, while having forced the United States to negotiate, remained both very conscious of its relative military weakness and contemptuous of Western resolve.

Seeking to sustain its newly won image as a major power, it feared that concessions at the negotiations would undermine that image. On the night of August 22–23 the Communists claimed that a UNC plane had attacked the conference site, impeded any investigation of the alleged attack, and then broke off negotiations.

Meanwhile, in late July General Van Fleet had decided to mount a series of attacks to seize positions three to seven miles above the KANSAS-WYOMING Line. These attacks had three objectives: keep the Communists off balance, probe Communist positions, and maintain an aggressive spirit in Eighth Army.

From August to September the X Corps and ROK I Corps in east central Korea fought bloody battles against tenacious KPA defenders to take objectives such as the Punchbowl, Bloody Ridge, and Heartbreak Ridge.

In west central Korea, the I and IX Corps attacked in October to seize new positions and had to defeat a tenacious CPVF defense to take their objectives. Van Fleet proposed a follow-on offensive, but the heavy casualties UNC units had taken in the recent limited attacks dissuaded Ridgway; he first postponed and then canceled the operation.

Armistice negotiations resumed on October 25, this time at Panmunjom, a tiny village southeast of Kaesong. Hope for an early armistice grew on November 27: the two delegations agreed that a line of demarcation for an armistice would be the existing line of contact, provided the belligerents reached an armistice within thirty days.

Hence, while both sides awaited the outcome of negotiations, fighting during the remainder of 1951 tapered off to patrol clashes, raids, and small battles for possession of outposts in No Man's Land.

On November 12 Ridgway had directed Van Fleet to assume an "active defense"; the Eighth Army was to establish an outpost line forward of its current main line of resistance, fortify both lines, patrol aggressively, and use its firepower to inflict maximum casualties on the enemy.

Van Fleet could counterattack to retake lost positions but could not mount any further multidivision operations without Ridgway's permission.

Discord over several issues, including the exchange of prisoners of war, prevented an armistice within the stipulated thirty days. The pris During the Panmunjom cease-fire talks, Col. James Murray, Jr., USMC, and Col. Chang Chun San, KPA, initial maps showing the north and south boundaries of the demarcation zone.

Thousands of Korean prisoners held by the UNC were actually South Koreans impressed into the KPA in 1950, and thousands of Chinese prisoners were former Nationalist soldiers impressed into the People's Liberation Army after the Chinese Civil War.

Most of these men had no desire to return to the DPRK or the PRC, and their refusal to do so would be a dramatic propaganda victory for the Western bloc.

American leaders, recalling Stalin's brutal treatment of Soviet soldiers taken prisoner by the Germans and returned to the USSR by the United States after World War II, also believed that voluntary repatriation was the moral course.

The Communist delegates protested vigorously that this was a violation of the Geneva Conventions of 1949. The resulting impasse deadlocked the negotiations until 1953.

The Communists opened another front on the prisoner issue on May 7, 1952. Communists held in the UNC prison camp on Koje-do, on orders smuggled to them from North Korea, lured the U.S. camp commander to a compound gate and dragged him inside.

The strategy, which became clear in subsequent prisoner demands, was to trade the officer's life and release for UNC admissions of inhumane treatment of captives, including alleged cruelties during previous screenings of prisoners in which a large number of prisoners refused repatriation. The obvious objective was to discredit the voluntary repatriation stand the UNC delegation had taken at Panmunjom.

Although a new camp commander secured his predecessor's release, in the process he signed a damaging statement including an admission that "there have been instances of bloodshed where many prisoners of war have been killed and wounded by U.N. Forces."

(There had been numerous violent incidents in the poorly designed and poorly run camp, and the Communists exploited the statement widely at Panmunjom and elsewhere for its propaganda value.)

Amid the Koje-do trouble, General Ridgway left Tokyo to replace General of the Army Dwight D. Eisenhower as the NATO Supreme Commander. Ridgway's replacement was General Mark W. Clark, Chief, Army Field Forces.

Clark became the new commander in the Far East, with one less responsibility than MacArthur and Ridgway had carried. On April 28, 1952, a peace treaty with Japan had gone into KOJE-DO

In January 1951 the Eighth Army established a prison camp on Koje-do, an island off the southern coast of Korea. By May 1952 the camp held approximately 170,000 prisoners of war and civilian internees in poorly designed facilities, and it had been assigned a disproportionately high percentage of low-quality U.S. and ROK personnel.

Eighth Army paid little attention to the camp even after a number of riots between Communist and anti-Communist prisoners and clashes between Communist prisoners and guards.

After General Boatner reestablished control over the camp in June 1952, General Clark relieved the Eighth Army of responsibility for prisoners of war and most of those held on Koje-do were moved to new, better-designed camps.

Faced immediately with the Koje-do affair, General Clark repudiated the prison camp commander's statement and placed Brig. Gen. Haydon L. Boatner, one of the U.S. Army's old China hands, in charge of the camp.

Clark ordered Boatner to move the prisoners into smaller, more manageable compounds and to institute other measures that would eliminate the likelihood of another uprising. General Boatner, in a carefully planned series of actions using tanks and infantry, crushed Communist resistance at the camp and completed the task in June.

In the United States, the growing unpopularity of the war made limiting casualties a key objective for Eighth Army. General Van Fleet successfully argued for a major expansion of the ROK Army, and he devoted much attention to strengthening the ROK Army's greatest weaknesses during the war's first year: inadequate training and poor leadership.

While the number of U.S. divisions in Korea did not drop until after the war, the growing number of ROK divisions, and their higherquality, allowed the Eighth Army to gradually turn over more of its front to ROK units and keep U.S. divisions in reserve for longer periods.

Because even limited attacks had produced high casualties in relation to the ground gained, the Eighth Army restricted subordinate commanders' freedom to attack. Since it could not pressure the enemy with ground attacks, the UNC turned to an "air pressure" campaign, striking at targets across North Korea.

The Far East Air Forces also mounted a renewed interdiction campaign against Communist supply lines, but the effort failed to prevent the CPVF and the KPA from receiving large amounts of artillery from the USSR.

At the start of 1952 the Communist forces had 71 artillery battalions with an estimated 852 guns at the front and an additional 361 battalions and 3,500 guns just to their rear to defend against UN breakthroughs.

By October 1952 they had something around 131 artillery battalions with 1,300 guns at the front and another 383 battalions and 4,000 guns just behind. The Communists used these weapons and their willingness to suffer, according to Western standards, exorbitant casualties to exert tremendous pressure on the UNC. From July to December 1952 CPVF and KPA units assaulted UNC outposts using their own version of meat grinder tactics.

The resulting battles, at hills UNC troops gave nicknames such as Old Baldy, the Hook, White Horse, and Reno, were small in scale compared to the war's first year.

The intensity of the combat for soldiers, however, rivaled that of World War I, with terrific artillery bombardments and hand-to-hand fighting in trenches. Between these assaults, both sides harassed each other with artillery fire and sent out patrols to contest the area between the opposing lines.

As this war of posts continued, the U.S. Army in 1952 was an institution in crisis. The opening of negotiations had erased the crisis atmosphere of 1950 and early 1951, and traditional fears about the dangers to the American economy from high military spending reasserted themselves.

President Truman and the Congress cut military spending and allocated a greater share of the defense budget to the Air Force to expand the nuclear deterrent force. These cuts, along with the decisions to institute an individual rotation policy in Korea and not to hold draftees and mobilized guardsmen and reservists for the duration of the war, left the Army unable to support all its commitments.

The service gave first priority in personnel to supporting the Eighth Army and second priority to supporting the Seventh Army in Germany, but commanders in both armies complained of serious declines in their units' proficiency.

In the continental United States, the manpower crisis crippled the Army's contribution to building an air defense system, nearly destroyed the service's training system, and by the end of 1952 had once again ruined the General Reserve (of its seven divisions, only the 82d Airborne was ready for use).

While the manpower crisis had negative effects on units, it did force the Army finally to comply with President Truman's 1948 order to end racial segregation. With only a partial mobilization for war and high casualties in Korea, racial segregation began to break down in the Eighth Army during 1950 as some commanders accepted any replacements they could obtain. In 1951 the Army began a racial integration program for units in Korea and extended it to the rest of the service later in the war.

In November the American people elected Dwight D. Eisenhower as the next President. A major issue in the campaign had been the war in Korea; and in a pledge to "go to Korea,"

Eisenhower implied that if elected he would attempt to end the war quickly. Consequently, when the President-elect in early December fulfilled his promise to visit Korea, there was indeed some expectation of a dramatic change in the conduct of the war.

In October General Clark had proposed a plan to obtain a military victory; it required extensive reinforcements for the UNC, a ground offensive supported by amphibious and airborne operations, air and naval attacks on targets in China, and possible use of nuclear weapons.

But it quickly became clear that Eisenhower, like President Truman, considered the costs of such an operation unacceptable and that he also preferred to seek an honorable armistice.

A UNC proposal in February 1953 that the two sides exchange sick and wounded prisoners initially brought no Communist response, but on March 5 Stalin died. The Soviet Politburo wanted an end to the high costs of supplying the Chinese and North Koreans; and without Soviet supplies and air power, the CPVF and the KPA would become vulnerable to a UNC offensive.

On March 28 the Communists favorably replied to the February proposal and also suggested that this exchange perhaps could "lead to the smooth settlement of the entirequestion of prisoners of war."

With that, the armistice conference resumed in April. An exchange of sick and wounded prisoners was carried out that same month, and on June 4 the Communist negotiators conceded on the issue of voluntary repatriation of prisoners.

During the spring of 1953 the Eighth Army fought some of the bloodiest battles of the outpost war as the CPVF and the KPA launched attacks to maintain pressure on the UNC and to take attention away from the concessions made at Panmunjom.

UNC units grimly defended some positions, but Lt. Gen. Maxwell D. Taylor, who had succeeded Van Fleet as the Eighth Army's commander in February, ordered others abandoned when it appeared that the enemy was willing to pay any price to take them.

Concerned over the steep increase in American casualties and aware that an armistice was imminent, Taylor decided that the costs of holding such outposts outweighed any tactical benefits. The enemy paid particular attention to ROK units, and on June 10 the CPVF attacked the five ROK divisions in the Kumsong salient in east central Korea.

Outnumbered, the ROK forces were pushed back an average of three kilometers across the salient before the CPVF broke off the attack, but their performance demonstrated a great improvement over that of ROK units under comparable conditions in the spring of 1951.

The UNC also sought to pressure its opponent, by bombing irrigation dams in North Korea but found ROK President Rhee as great a problem when on June 18 he ordered the release of over 25,000 Korean prisoners, many of them Southerners impressed into the KPA, who had refused repatriation.

Rhee had long opposed any armistice that left the peninsula divided and had made threats to remove ROK forces from UNC control. He also feared that with an armistice the ROK would lose the support and protection of the United States, especially if the United States withdrew all its ground forces.

In the end Rhee backed down when the U.S. government suggested that it would sign a mutual defense treaty with the ROK and provide it with significant economic and military assistance.

Furious over the release of the prisoners, the Communists decided to teach Rhee a lesson before concluding the armistice negotiations. On July 13 the CPVF attacked the Kumsong salient in greater strength than in June.

Shattering one division, the attack forced the ROK units to withdraw south of the Kumsong River. Again the ROK units' performance showed that this army had greatly improved since 1951.

General Taylor on July 16 ordered the ROK II Corps, with U.S. air and artillery support, to counterattack; but he halted the operation on July 20 short of the original line since by that date the armistice delegations had come to a new accord and needed only to work out a few small details. Taylor's order to halt ended the last major battle of the war.

After a week of dealing with administrative matters, each chief delegate signed the military armistice at Panmunjom at 10:00 A.M. on July 27; later that day General Clark and the enemy commanders affixed their signatures to the agreement. As stipulated in the agreement, all fighting stopped twelve hours after the first signing, at 10:00 P.M., July 27, 1953.

Thirty-seven months of fighting had exacted a high toll. South Korea had lost over 187,000 soldiers dead, an estimated 30,000 missing, and about 429,000 wounded. South Korea's civilians also had suffered greatly: estimates of the dead and missing range from 500,000 to 1 million. Up to 1.5 million North Korean soldiers and civilians died in the war.

Chapter 5: The Aftermath Of The War

By the terms of the armistice, the line of demarcation between North and South Korea closely approximated the front line as it existed at the final hour and represented a relatively small adjustment of the prewar division.

Within three days of the signing of the armistice, each opposing force withdrew two kilometers from this line to establish a demilitarized zone.

The armistice provisions forbade either force to bring additional troops or new weapons into Korea, although replacement one for one and in kind was permissible.

To oversee the enforcement of all armistice terms and to negotiate resolution of any violations, the armistice established a Military Armistice Commission composed of an equal number of officers from the UN Command, China, South Korea, and North Korea.

This body was assisted by the Neutral Nations Supervisory Commission whose members came from Sweden, Switzerland, Czechoslovakia, and Poland. Representatives of those same countries, with India furnishing an umpire and custodial forces, formed the Neutral Nations Repatriation Commission to handle the disposition of prisoners refusing repatriation.

Finally, a provision of the armistice recommended that the belligerent governments convene a political conference to negotiate a final political settlement of the whole Koreanquestion.

By September 6 all prisoners wishing to be repatriated had been exchanged. From the UNC returnees came full details of brutally harsh treatment—murder, torture, and starvation in enemy prison camps and of an extensive Communist political indoctrination program designed to produce prisoner collaboration. Several hundred

U.S.returnees were investigated on charges of collaborating with the enemy, but few were convicted.

The transfer of nonrepatriates to the Neutral Nations Repatriation Commission came next. In the drawn-out procedure that followed, few of the prisoners changed their minds as officials from both sides attempted to convince former members of their respective commands that they should return home.

Of twenty-three Americans who at first refused repatriation, two decided to return. On February 1, 1954, the Neutral Nations Repatriation Commission dissolved itself after releasing the last of the nonrepatriates as civilians free to choose their own destinations.

The main scene then shifted to Geneva, Switzerland, where the political conference recommended in the armistice agreement convened on April 26.

There was a complete impasse from the beginning: the representatives of UNC member nations wanted to reunify Korea through UN-supervised elections; the Communist delegation refused to recognize the United Nations' authority to deal with the matter.

The conference on Korea closed June 15. Leaving Korea divided essentially along the prewar line, the Geneva impasse merely reestablished the prewar confrontation between the two Korean governments. However, the ROK now had a military vastly increased in size and ability and the United States had promised the ROK huge amounts of economic and military aid.

Later in 1954 the United States would sign a mutual defense treaty with the ROK; and the Eighth Army, although reduced to two U.S. divisions, would remain in Korea.

The war's impact reached far beyond Korea. Despite criticism of the armistice by those who agreed with General MacArthur that there was no substitute for victory, the UNC had upheld the principle of suppressing armed aggression.

True, the Security Council had been able to enlist forces under the UN banner in June 1950 only in the absence of the USSR veto. Nevertheless, the UNC success strengthened the possibility of keeping or restoring peace through the UN machinery, at the General Assembly.

For China, the war brought several benefits. It had maintained in the DPRK a buffer state on its sensitive northern border. Soviet assistance, especially in improving the Chinese army and air force, gave China a more powerful military posture at war's end than when it had intervened. Its performance in Korea, despite vast losses, won China respect as a nation to be reckoned with, not only in Asian but also in world affairs.

For the United States, the war brought a major change in its containment strategy against the USSR. Instead of relying principally on economic and political tools backed by a small nuclear deterrent force, containment's emphasis shifted during the war to military means.

While Eisenhower did reduce military spending after the war, the U.S. armed forces remained much larger than they had been in 1950, possessed many more and increasingly powerful nuclear weapons, and were ensured a steady supply of manpower through the retention of conscription.

Chapter 6: The Divided Peninsula Goes To War

A strong case can be made that the Empire of Japan made its largest mistake even as it determined to bomb Pearl Harbor, Hawaii, on December seventh, 1941. This brash motion awoke the sleeping large of the United States. And quickly thereafter, Japan — which had formerly appeared almost unstoppable — have become forced to make a protracted, protracted retreat once more to their domestic islands inside the Pacific.

In the preliminary aftermath of Pearl Harbor, Japanese forces regarded to be in the ascendancy, seizing the American-controlled Philippines together with severa British and French possessions in Southeast Asia but the U.S. Doggedly driven lower back towards the Japanese, combating them off of island after island, inch after inch, farther and farther back into the Pacific. And after Japan's defeat through U.S. Forces on the Battle of Midway in 1942, the

American surge inexorably pushed onward within the path of the Japanese mainland itself. But in advance than Japan turned into overrun by Allied troops, the question arose as to what have to be done with the Japanese ownership of Korea. The Allied powers have been truly no longer going to permit Japan to preserve it – so what ought to be accomplished?

At the Yalta Conference in February of 1945, Korea's future and plans for the rest of the postwar Pacific were mentioned. Among the Allied leaders of the battle – america, the Soviet Union, and Britain – it modified into Soviet chief Joseph Stalin who made his intentions smooth. Stalin needed to establish a "joint trusteeship" of Korea, which is probably led by way of the use of the Russians and the Americans. Stalin felt that a newly freed Korea might no longer be capable of stand on its non-public and may want to be "mentored" with the useful resource of the Allies.

The Americans have been not almost as concerned about Russian affect in Korea as they have been approximately capability Russian have an effect on in Japan. The consensus inside the kingdom department grow to be that it might be in the extraordinary hobbies of the us to stress Japan to give up earlier than Russian troops have been deployed onto Japanese soil, due to the fact if Russian troops participated in Japan's defeat, they will need to be accorded an profession area. This could have introduced on Japan being break up into North Japan and South Japan, and American planners needed to keep away from this.

Furthermore, they knew that the Soviets might be tied up with Japanese troops that have been already within the Manchurian region of Northeast China and North Korea, just so they desired to permit the Russians stay preoccupied with those regions even as

America handled mainland Japan on their very very own.

Unfortunately, the essential aspect to forcing a quicker surrender with Japan came via the usage of nuclear weapons. The atomic bomb – even though it have turn out to be a low-yield nuclear tool – become devastating enough to obliterate entire towns.

Shortly after one of these bombs changed into delivered to the Japanese city of Hiroshima on August 6th, accompanied thru a second bomb dropped on August 9th, 1945, the Soviet Union formally declared struggle on Japan. With the Soviets preventing the Japanese in Manchuria and North Korea, the frenzy changed into now right now to get the Japanese to capitulate in advance than the Soviets need to benefit get proper of entry to to Japan itself.

Under splendid pressure, on August fifteenth, 1945, Japan ultimately introduced its motive to surrender and might formally capitulate to the United States on September 2d. The Soviets were on cleanup obligation in Manchuria and North Korea, and the usa on my own changed into coping with affairs in Japan itself. Korea may be split along Soviet and U.S. Spheres of have an effect on at the 38th parallel.

Communist shops had already been gift at the Korean Peninsula and had been one of the thorns inside the component of Japanese career. And now, with the communist electricity of Soviet Russia controlling all territory north of the 38th parallel, it changed into nice natural for North Korea to end up a communist state. Under the guidance of the U.S., within the period in-between, South Korea changed into converted proper right into a capitalist democratic republic.

But despite the fact that those Koreas had been separated through the thirty eighth parallel, neither one modified into inclined to certainly accept this branch, and every government vied for dominance over everything of the peninsula. The communist North took the initiative with the useful useful resource of transferring south over the 38th parallel on June 25th, 1950.

The attack started out inside the early morning hours while South Korean troops placed on the border have been hit with unexpected mortar and artillery hearth. The next trouble they knew, the South Korean troops had been then literally run over thru the usage of the advancing communists, who despatched some a hundred fifty tanks and different heavily armored cars rolling into South Korea. This became finished at the orders of North Korean leader Kim Il-sung, the founder of the communist Kim dynasty that have been mounted with the aid of the usage of the usage of the Russians at the forestall of World War II. Kim Il-sung, it's important to be conscious, is the grandfather of the cutting-edge North

Korean leader (as of this writing) Kim Jong-un.

The forces of Kim Il-sung were ruthless of their march on South Korea, and seemingly hoped to take over the southern part of the Korean Peninsula so unexpectedly that the world is probably too taken aback to reply. The international became virtually amazed. Before the invasion, the top U.S. Army reliable inside the vicinity, General Douglas MacArthur, grow to be happy that North Korea didn't have the audacity to strive a seizure of the south through force. He became incorrect.

But irrespective of how audacious the North Koreans have been, they weren't going to break out with such an incursion so without problems, and their movements provoked a right away reaction from the newly hooked up United Nations. This delivered about a U.N.-sponsored coalition (led through the us) being mobilized in South Korea to repulse the North Koreans.

Initially, subjects did not pass so nicely for the safety of South Korea. Even as quickly as U.N. Troops arrived, the North Koreans placed up this shape of fierce offensive that very little ground have come to be obtained. And with their backs up towards the wall (or in this situation, up in competition to the sea), U.S.-led forces had been driven decrease returned in the back of the so-known as "Pusan Perimeter." This changed into a protective line which have become hooked up around the southern port city of Pusan. It have come to be essentially pleasant a toehold that the outnumbered U.S.-led forces clung to because the surging North Koreans tried to force them into the ocean. However, the Americans maintained air supremacy, bombing North Korean positions at will. Nevertheless, even below heavy bombardment, the North Koreans driven in competition to the Pusan Perimeter and have been able to interrupt via factors of this protecting line to strike at U.S./U.N. Troop positions. But no matter all of these repeated incursions and with the assist of the U.S. Marines, the line stayed by using the usage of and massive intact, preventing the North Koreans from touchdown a knockout blow.

The maximum first-rate attempt of the North Koreans to gain a few traction happened in early September at some level inside the notorious Naktong Offensive, wherein U.S. Troops received heavy casualties however nevertheless controlled to repel the North Koreans. This stabilization of protecting traces become pivotal for the capability of the U.N. To ship reinforcements, 70,000 of which arrived on September fifteenth.

The troops were deployed within the port metropolis of Inchon clearly 25 miles southwest of Seoul, South Korea, which become occupied by means of the North Koreans at that factor. This end up outside of the Pusan Perimeter and furnished a unstable logistical venture. However,

General MacArthur had a stoop that such a landing would possibly display strategically pivotal in gaining the better hand. If finished proper, he believed that sparkling troops deployed at Inchon may moreover want to get in the again of the troops that had been already assailing the Pusan Perimeter and thereby create a state of affairs in which the North Koreans were sandwiched.

This glowing batch of troops located themselves spherical Seoul, and while the North Korean squaddies at the Pusan Perimeter tried to intercept them, the U.S./U.N. Troops stationed at Pusan drove beforehand and attacked the North Koreans from in the again of.

Chapter 7: North Korea At The Rebound

The U.S.-led U.N. Troops have been simplest imagined to pressure the North Koreans out of South Korea, but after they had been at the run, the Americans endured to increase. In the delight of this rate, General MacArthur even went up to now as to talk about driving the North Koreans all the manner as lots as the Yalu River, which marked the border amongst North Korea and China. This have turn out to be obviously more than the U.N. Had to begin with deliberate.

It moreover should probably bring about World War III, considering the truth that China made it easy that if U.S. Troops got here close to Chinese territory, they – along element their Soviet allies – could grow to be right now involved. Chinese troops were already being secretly despatched into Korea, however open involvement may be an superb statement of war with the beneficial aid of China.

These issues inspired President Truman to hassle a unique directive to General MacArthur. He knowledgeable him that he changed into snug with U.S. Troops crossing the 38th parallel, however he warned the overall to drag lower again if Chinese or Soviet forces had been to project the U.S. Presence. MacArthur changed into not of a thoughts to pay this any heed.

In mid-October, Chinese troops commenced out to pass the Yalu River to sign up for North Korean warring parties within the face of the American enhance. Truman, within the interim, summoned MacArthur to fulfill with him on close by Wake Island, out within the Pacific. MacArthur, as though he had been drastically displeased to be disturbed with the resource of his private president, became stated to have had a contemptuous and condescending disposition sooner or later of the assembly, and treated President Truman greater as an intruder than the Commander in Chief.

As an extended manner as General MacArthur have become concerned, he modified into the individual in price and he didn't want everyone else – even the President of america – interfering alongside together along with his affairs. President Truman, inside the interim, left the assembly glad that MacArthur had long past simply electricity-mad. The popular turn out to be truly the only decide inside the Pacific theater; he have emerge as the person in rate of occupied Japan and have become now moreover principal the charge towards North Korea.

Truman, even though he valued MacArthur's strategic knowledge, modified into worried about the overall's capability to emerge as a loose cannon. Nevertheless, with no person to update him, General MacArthur might preserve in his feature of predominant the warfare attempt in Korea within the in the meantime. And on October 20th, five days after this fateful assembly,

U.S. Forces drove into Pyongyang – North Korea's capital metropolis.

Just some days later, but, battalions of South Korean troops positioned within the location have been hit through devices sent from China. The Chinese wielded heavy firepower in a blistering attack that drove the South Koreans decrease lower back. This attack became accompanied up by means of the usage of an assault completed thru some 20,000 Chinese troops on the U.S./U.N. Positions throughout the town of Unsan.

This assault completely destroyed the defenders; many have been killed inside the exchange and people who lived to appearance some exclusive day had been pressured once more approximately 15 miles farther south. General MacArthur spoke back to this attack with the resource of sending U.S. Aircraft on bombing runs all during the Korean section of the Yalu, blowing up electricity plants and fantastic important installations. This circulate did now not sit too nicely with President Truman, who endured to worry that MacArthur had lengthy past too a long way and might provoke the Chinese.

For those once more home at the State Department, it seemed that MacArthur had gone rogue. U.S. Officers had together decided that some aspect need to be completed however Truman hesitated, not wishing to dispose of this form of awesome favored right in the center of a conflict. General MacArthur, within the intervening time, modified into taking decisive action.

In November, MacArthur moved his troops into offensive positions toward the North, but they ended up becoming ensnared through the enemy, which emerge as strategically positioned all spherical them. On the night time time time of November twenty fifth, the Chinese launched their ferocious assault toward MacArthur's Eighth Army. In this melee, a few 4000 U.S. Troops had been killed, drastically injured, or taken prisoner. The U.S. Forces within the vicinity have been then knocked backward with wave after wave of Chinese infantrymen coming for them.

It's nicely well worth noting that China is the maximum populous u.S.A. On the earth nowadays, and this come to be actual in MacArthur's day, as well. This modified proper right into a fact that China most truly used to its fullest gain all through the Korean War. Communist leader Mao Zedong himself frequently joked approximately simply how expendable he believed China's massive population to be. He as quick as even remarked that China need to live to tell the tale a nuclear war truly because it had such a number of humans that the usa of america could be able to soak up big casualties.

It is a lovable issue to should face an navy with a reputedly in no way-finishing deliver of troops, mainly at the same time as their communist commanders had this kind of callous brush aside even as it came to dropping their blood. The lousy interest of surely what they were up in competition to commenced to take its toll on the U.S./U.N. Forces.

The Eighth Army became being battered via the infinite drift of Chinese fighters, and it changed into feared that the advancing Chinese must quickly encircle them in a pincer maneuver. As such, they determined to withdraw while they in spite of the reality that had the danger to perform that. This added approximately a massive convoy retreating down one of the few routes left useable, again to South Korea, on November thirtieth, 1950.

Unfortunately for them, the Chinese had already anticipated this flow into, and had located gunmen and artillery within the mountainous regions above the pass. As the American troops fled south, that that they had no choice but to run the gauntlet via a bombardment of bullets and mortars hurled at them from all sides. It wasn't prolonged in advance than they have been struggling high casualties.

And making subjects worse, the street soon have end up blocked with the aid of manner of automobiles that have been blown up thru the Chinese. This compelled troops to need to bypass walking underneath heavy gunfire truely to get thru the wreckage. Fortunately for the determined troops at the floor, the U.S. Air Force came to their rescue, bombing the Chinese positions from the air.

U.S. Air dominance controlled to break the stranglehold the Chinese held on the skip. This short beginning become then accompanied through a price of U.S. Floor forces on the Chinese, a flow that forced the Chinese troops to retreat. Finally, the U.S.

Chapter 8: Regroup And Rethink

General MacArthur had promised his guys that their victory modified into impending and that they may moreover be home for Christmas. But the month of December had already arrived and the battered remnants of U.S. Forces had been driven decrease decrease lower back into South Korea, huddled across the metropolis of Seoul, pretty loads wherein that they'd started. It changed right right into a blow to morale, to say the least.

But the influx of Chinese troops into the struggle became a real pastime-changer. The Chinese forces were bold and warfare-hardened. China were in a near-ordinary kingdom of war for many years. In the Nineteen Thirties, Japan had launched an invasion of China, even even as China itself become locked in a civil struggle amongst Chinese nationalists and Chinese communists. The nationalists and communists have been compelled to enter right into a truce with every awesome to take on the outdoor threat of the Japanese.

As brief as Japan end up defeated in 1945, but, the conflict most of the Chinese factions become once more on. The communists have been in the end a success, putting in place communist rule over China within the fall of 1949. It end up a good buy tons much less than a yr later that those veteran combatants had been despatched to stand off in competition to the U.S.-subsidized forces of South Korea in the summer time of 1950.

Faced with this onslaught, the U.S./U.N. Forces desperately needed to regroup and rethink their technique. After carefully considering their alternatives, the U.S./U.N. Troops launched a renewed attack on the North in February of 1951. Units have been stationed across the cities of Wonju and Chipyongni and tasked with preserving the perimeter. It wasn't lengthy into this skirmish that the Chinese all all over again advanced and tried to encircle the defenders.

At one point, the Chinese regarded as despite the fact that they were approximately to interrupt thru the strains, however a U.N. Unit composed in particular of French troops poured into the breach and were capable of combat the Chinese off. And then – right at the equal time because it seemed that the Chinese had been about to get the pinnacle hand towards the U.N. Fighters all over again – the U.S. Air Force got here roaring overhead and all yet again obliterated the Chinese positions on the ground.

This proved to be too much for the Chinese, and eventually precipitated their withdrawal on February 14th, predominant to the number one easy victory of U.S.-led forces in the direction of the Chinese troops. After their defeat, U.S./U.N. Troops solidified their keep over Seoul and have been speedy marching again as tons as the 38th parallel.

The troop positions had progressed and the Allied attempt come to be doing better closer to the stressful conditions they confronted, however President Truman come to be although significantly disturbed at General MacArthur's seeming unwillingness to heed his directives. Alarmingly, MacArthur had in recent times made feedback about bombing mainland China. He additionally mentioned bringing within the Chinese nationalist forces that have been even though holed up in Taiwan. Truman idea that such speak changed into reckless, to mention the least, and could probable result in Soviet intervention – if not World War III.

Yes, Harry Truman, the president who dropped nuclear bombs on Japan in 1945, had come to take the risk of igniting a international conflagration very extensively. In this supposedly confined "police movement" in Korea, Truman favored for cautious, measured motion coupled with restraint. Douglas MacArthur have become a unfastened cannon and the stakes had been excessive enough that Harry Truman just couldn't danger setting him off. Truman ended up firing MacArthur in April of 1951. It became a hard name to make, however Truman determined it needed to be executed. General Matthew Ridgeway would probably update MacArthur.

The Chinese, within the period in-between, had regrouped and launched every one-of-a-kind primary offensive on May sixteenth, which comprised some 38,000 North Koreans and 137,000 Chinese troops. The enemy forces came smashing down on the South Korean and American troops. This time round, but, the U.S./U.N. Forces had observed out a few pretty valuable instructions about the methods in their adversaries.

Initially, they had been driven decrease again thru the Chinese, but after a sequence of fierce skirmishes, the North Koreans overextended their strains. Seizing the possibility, the U.S. Eighth Army struck lower back and become succesful to interrupt thru North Korean traces, inflicting a immoderate variety of causalities. This decisive defeat appeared to bring China once more to the negotiating table, and by means of manner of June they have been sending out feelers to the United Nations that they were interested in commencing a communicate.

The subsequent month observed a prime lull in preventing while the two facets entered into reliable talks. Initially, the discussion changed into promising, and on November twenty seventh, 1951, a initial armistice line turn out to be already in interest. The talks commenced out to interrupt down swiftly after this milestone become reached, however, and preventing all all yet again resumed.

The subsequent section of the warfare took on a form of unnecessary collection of decrease returned-and-forth skirmishes wherein both factors struggled to preserve immediately to their positions in what had become a bloody stalemate. Both factors preferred to give up the carnage, but achieving an settlement to stop the war become tough in the detrimental climate of the Cold War, and each aspect felt like they in reality had too much to lose if they gave up any ground.

The warfare, you note, became a first rate deal larger than simply the Korean Peninsula itself. The vital hassle turn out to be what awesome countries may additionally fall if this one domino came tumbling down. The United States didn't want to offer any concessions out of situation that they may cause an escalation in provocations via communist forces in different components of the globe. North Korea didn't want to concede too much either, for the motive that North Koreans desired to save face with their communist allies.

It wasn't till 1952 that the peace talks began to make some headway, with every additives agreeing to create a postwar demilitarized location (DMZ) to split the north and south in fact above the thirty eighth parallel. It is as an possibility sudden to keep in mind all of the folks that died for every facets to come to be proper wherein they began out. It's particularly absurd for the North Koreans who started the conflict. At the surrender of the day, masses of masses North Koreans (in addition to Chinese troops) went to their graves simplest for the line of demarcation to live proper in which it had been previous to the invasion.

Nevertheless, the conflict had taken on an additional size within the Cold War, and each facets had been content material fabric if they may simply keep sufficient face to get matters back to in which they had been in advance than the hostilities started. But even as soon as this bypass once more to the recognition quo changed into agreed upon, one of the ultimate sticking elements emerge as over what to do with all the prisoners of war every facet had received.

One of the big issues that arose was that some of the North Korean prisoners had made it easy that they did now not want to go again to communist-run North Korea. Despite this, North Korean officials insisted that all North Korean prisoners be again. They claimed that the North Korean troops were became in the direction of communism thru their captors.

In all probability, but, the North Korean defectors in reality observed the possibility for a better existence outside of communism and that they went for it. Nevertheless, their very personal troops refusing to go back domestic became considered as a severe blow to Marxist ideology, and North Korea's regime wanted to avoid such embarrassment. But the U.N. Remained firm in this factor and insisted that any POWs who desired asylum can be granted the right to live in South Korea or gather steady haven in Taiwan.

Further complicating subjects, it have become determined that some 16,000 of the meant "North Korean" POWs had been in reality South Korean citizens who had formerly been detained by using using the North Koreans and forced to combat for the North Korean forces.

North Korea additionally had hassle on the same time because it came to plans for returning U.S./U.N. Troops they were suspected to be maintaining. When pressured to take account of the POWs that they held, the North Koreans produced a listing that fantastic indicated eleven,559 prisoners presently of their possession. This became complex, due to the truth that in keeping with the U.N.'s meticulous report-retaining, this turn out to be simplest a small fraction of the men who had long past lacking in movement. Where were the relaxation of the missing troops?

Many have been absolute confidence killed, in direct violation of Geneva Conventions regarding the remedy of prisoners of struggle. Others in reality perished from the rampant contamination and disorder positioned in the negative sanitation conditions of the facilities wherein they have been held. Still others, however, were being kept for propaganda functions. It's unsettling to suppose that POWs want to actually vanish into the clutches of communist North Korea, but it actually did display up. This became dramatically established in 1994, even as Korean warfare veteran Cho Chang-ho (who become presumed useless) managed to break out and inform the arena all about it.

But probable even more traumatic had been the American troops who have been subjected to brainwashing by manner of using North Korean and Chinese communists. Incidentally, the term "brainwashing" definitely originates from the unique remedy American POWs obtained from the communists. Whatever this entailed, for a few American POWs it modified into powerful, due to the fact in July of 1953, on the struggle's stop, at the least 21 POWs publicly made a declaration that they decided on to live permanently in communist-run society.

According to U.S. Officials, the ones guys have been brainwashed, in spite of the reality that others nowadays may additionally moreover argue that they surely made a desire in their own volition. Nevertheless, the perception that the foxy communists can also want to govern the minds of inclined Americans have turn out to be an indicator of the Cold War. Even Hollywood immortalized this challenge depend with wartime movies on the aspect of The Manchurian Candidate based totally upon the ebook of the equal name, which depicted the reviews of brainwashed POWs.

At any price, while the 2 components endured to bicker and feud over the future of their POWs, the bloody siege on every components persevered to play out. And with the beneficial aid of the fall of 1952, the situation was having a right away impact on that 365 days's presidential election. President Harry Truman's Democratic Party become getting hit tough thru the Republicans, who lambasted the Truman manage as being too indecisive in finishing the conflict. Truman himself, sensing absolutely how a whole lot of a legal responsibility Korea changed into for him, definitely opted no longer to run for reelection.

Chapter 9: The Art Of Ignoring War

With Eisenhower's election, many had been hoping that this change in Washington may bring about a trade in how the U.S. approached the conflict in Korea. Soon after President Eisenhower became sworn in in 1953, he did truly change U.S. Coverage – but not lots within the course of Korea as China. In particular, Eisenhower made it diagnosed that he wasn't satisfied that the Chinese Civil War that had introduced the place the Chinese communist authorities within the first area became absolutely over.

China, you word, had fought a knock-down, drag-out fight among a communist faction led through Mao Zedong and so-called "nationalists" led with the aid of the forces of Chiang Kai-shek. Initially, the nationalists had the gain however after being forced to fight off the Japanese in a few unspecified time inside the future of World War II, plenty of their electricity were sapped. Then right now after the war, at the same time as Mao's communist guerillas actually got here down from the mountains wherein they have been hiding, they had been capable of whittle away at the nationalists till they had been compelled to escape.

By 1949, the nationalists had been pushed all of the manner off the mainland and pressured to evacuate to the close by island of Taiwan, wherein they set up a ultra-modern base of operations that might grow to be the kingdom of Taiwan – a free, unbiased u.S. Of the us this is nevertheless in lifestyles (as of this writing). With the nationalists exiled to Taiwan, the Chinese communists ultimately declared themselves the winners of the ideological battle and sought to get the world to understand the communist regime as the rightful controller of China's future.

In 1953, Eisenhower made it seemed that he didn't, and he allowed the nationalist government in Taiwan to start to revenue new assaults on mainland China. Eisenhower become a actual master statesman who discovered the big photo, and in the new president's thoughts, the Cold War conflict over the future of Korea had an immediate connection to Taiwan.

Eisenhower knew that if China especially modified into not installation check within the Korean struggle, Mao and his forces may want to maximum probably strive a takeover of Taiwan subsequent. And for simply anybody who's familiar with the bitter statistics among communist China and the democratic republic of Taiwan, it's smooth that if China were to invade, the bloodshed could be awesome.

President Eisenhower knew this, and so you can make China count on twice approximately this sort of skip, he meant to use Korea as his checkmate on this geopolitical struggle. Eisenhower, at this element in time, additionally firmly believed that such an escalation turned into the remarkable manner to hold China to the table – and he have become proper. Shortly thereafter, on February 8th, 1953, Mao issued a unprecedented public statement in which he proclaimed, "We choice peace, however so long as U.S. Imperialism does no longer discard its barbaric and unreasonable needs and its plots to increase its aggression, the resolution of the Chinese humans can fine be to preserve to combat together with the Korean humans to the quit."

Although the phrases are cloaked in ideological rhetoric, they signaled to the arena that Mao turn out to be sincerely prepared for peace. Mao become a pragmatist, and with a brand new president on the helm of the united states, for now he decided that the tremendous issue he have to do have turn out to be sit down and wait till he turned into moved to further motion.

The catalyst to transport Mao might come the following month, with the abrupt and unexpected dying of Soviet chief Joseph Stalin. Since China trusted course from Moscow, with the death of Stalin Mao come to be in huge factor on his very own. Stalin had formerly endorsed Mao to play a double activity in which he talked tough with the Americans and but become cautious to avoid a far wider conflict that might pull the Soviets into the aggregate. You see, the usa desired to avoid a third international warfare, and the Soviets were without a doubt as hesitant.

Historical revisionists have claimed that Stalin desired to spark World War III, however the truth is that he didn't even want World War II. Stalin turned into hesitant to get worried within the 2d international battle; Hitler forced his hand with the useful aid of right away invading Soviet Russia. It took Stalin even longer to assert battle on Japan; he remarkable took decisive movement a few weeks earlier than Japan surrendered in 1945.

Rather than engage in all-out battle, Stalin favored to apply proxies to combat his battles for him. If he might also need to get the Chinese or Koreans to combat the Americans which have become nice, but he favored to keep away from direct conflict amongst American and Soviet troops if possible. This choice to keep away from entanglement in Korea persisted after Stalin's loss of life, and it changed into his successors – the so-known as "Soviet troika" of Nikita Khrushchev, Georgy Malenkov, and Lavrentiy Beria – who in the long run happy Mao to wind down the Korean warfare.

Mao become in Moscow for Stalin's funeral in March while the Soviet Council of Ministers suggested him to take decisive movement to surrender the battle. Even so, U.S./U.N. Forces ramped up their hostilities within the resulting months, culminating in air raids in North Korea which blew up irrigation dams in mid-May. This brought approximately big damage as torrents of water burst forth, leaving brilliant swaths of Korean geographical place a flooded mess, ruining plants.

Chairman Mao desired to surrender the war, however he become decided to acquire this from a feature of strength – now not weak point. As counterproductive as it might appear, this led the peace-minded Mao to ramp up his very own assaults late in May. This entailed sending communist forces on numerous offensives aimed closer to accomplishing minor tactical objectives that could make an eventual cessation of stopping greater agreeable. This has become observed via a large offensive in July that driven decrease back South Korean forces severa miles.

Chapter 10: Aftermath Of The Armistice

In 2018, President Donald Trump modified into roundly ridiculed even as, absolutely earlier than a summit with North Korean leader Kim Jong-un, he described the Korean battle as "the longest war" and hinted that he can also broker a deal to ultimately quit it. Several articles suddenly surfaced to reality-check the Commander in Chief, talking of methods stupid the president come to be to explain a conflict that precipitated 1953 as although ongoing.

But in this example, the reality-checkers were given it incorrect. Ask any historian and they will inform you: the Korean war never ended. The armistice signed in 1953 became more or plenty less a truce that ended at once hostilities, however an reliable peace treaty to stop the conflict in no manner transpired. So in that enjoy, certain – the Korean conflict is honestly the longest warfare America has ever been part of, and it's miles technically but ongoing.

At the signing of the armistice that created the ceasefire/standoff among North and South Korea, the South Korean president, Syngman Rhee, come to be adamant about not accepting the division of Korea. At one trouble he even demanded that President Eisenhower dispose of U.S. Troops if he deliberate to sign an armistice just so South Korean forces can also need to combat on without him.

Rhee quick scaled once more his rhetoric, however but, he never in fact did receive the perception that the Korean Peninsula need to remain divided. He held out desire of an coming near near unification which might probably boot communist chief Kim Il-sung out of power in the north and create a capitalist, democratic republic spanning the whole Korean Peninsula.

On the alternative hand, if a real prevent to the Korean war changed into officially declared these days, it'd seem to legitimize the popularity quo of there being separate

Koreas, thereby nixing the notion that the peninsula could ever be unified. And in some ways, this sort of feat would probable simply paintings in North Korea's choice, granting it legitimacy as a separate communist nation.

At any fee, the armistice of 1953 stabilized the scenario, in no small aspect due to the truth the today's DMZ created a powerful line of safety with an fantastic array of South Korean troops reinforced with the beneficial resource of American squaddies. These defenders stood on defend (and preserve to face on guard) lest the North Koreans attempt any other invasion. As of this writing they've got no longer, and the standoff stays – with South Korean and North Korean troops sincerely status in the course of from each one-of-a-kind over the DMZ, 24 hours an afternoon, 7 days a week.

Immediately after the cessation of fighting, the usa persevered to shepherd and mould the evolution of South Korean democracy.

The U.S. Nearly out of vicinity South Korea to communism, and the consensus turned into that since it took plenty American blood and cash to maintain South Korea out of the communist orbit, then it higher be made as politically, economically, and socially sound as viable. These efforts were led through the USIS (United States Information Service) which modified into tasked with the continuing encouragement of democracy in the Republic of Korea.

It come to be under the aegis of the USIS that ratings of government officials, business business organisation moguls, and educators got here to South Korea to assist spread the beliefs of democratic governance. It modified into no smooth task. As come to be said inside the expert USIS assessment file from 1959, "Democracy is a philosophy alien to the Korean subculture; without the prolonged battles and robust convictions that punctuate the development of democracy inside the West, the Republic of Korea became created in a single day, in big detail in the Western image. The danger on this quick transition lies inside the possibility that having been made privy to a better lifestyles and the advantages of proper government, and having loved the advantages of neither, the Koreans may likely blame the failures on democracy while not having without a doubt professional nor absolutely understood it, with consequent rejection. The motive [of the USIS] is to promote information, to help Koreans in growing and strengthening their democratic institutions a good way to ward off this contingency."

Not all Koreans preferred having Western establishments of presidency foisted upon them, regardless of how plenty the USIS insisted that it changed into for their very personal ideal. Making topics even worse, the promised give up end result of democracy and capitalism have been now not right away obvious to maximum South Koreans. Immediately after the stop of the Korean battle, in fact, South Korea virtually located itself lagging in the lower back of North Korea economically. And at the democratic the front, South Korean President Syngman Rhee had emerge as increasingly more authoritarian in his rule, as rapid became apparent in his seeming refusal to step down from energy.

Initially, it were deemed that South Korean presidents have to most effective serve for two phrases, but in 1952, in reality after Rhee secured his 2nd time period, he had the time period restrict removed from South Korea's charter, which allowed him to run for a third term in 1956. The preference have become no longer a famous one, but Rhee controlled to win his 0.33 time period but the talk.

Rhee then ran over again in 1960 for a fourth time period, and actually obtained place of job in an uncontested election. The rival candidate, Cho Pyong-ok, had died some weeks earlier – leaving Rhee due to the fact the handiest dwelling candidate at the poll. Nevertheless, regardless of the truth that there was only one man or woman on the pinnacle of the charge tag to vote for, South Koreans became their interest to the vice chairman slot at the price tag. In South Korea, you spot, the V.P. Applicants are voted for one after the opportunity from the presidential candidates. This truth created the faint preference that Rhee can be elected with a V.P. From the competition birthday celebration.

With this in thoughts, there was a large turnout on election day to vote for Cho Pyong-right enough's V.P. Candidate, Chang Myon, over Rhee's V.P. Choose, Lee Ki Poong. The famous sentiment modified into honestly with Chang, but on the equal time as the voting effects got here out, they confirmed Rhee's V.P. With a whopping seventy nine.2% and Chang Myon with most effective 17.Five%. As new as maximum South Koreans had been to democracy, maximum of them had a sinking feeling that some component modified into incorrect with their election system.

They had a presidential candidate triumphing through using using landslide margins who then secured a fourth time period, uncontested. And despite the fact that most have emerge as out to vote for the oppositional vice presental candidate, all in their votes come what might also had been tabulated for Rhee's V.P. As an opportunity. Soon thereafter, accusations of a rigged election hit the streets, and wave after wave of protests rocked Seoul in overdue 1960 and early 1961, earlier than an outright coup have come to be staged to get the detested Rhee taken out of workplace for suitable.

Escorted distant places with the useful resource of using American CIA dealers,

Rhee end up compelled to flee to Hawaii. The former V. P. Candidate Chang Myong modified into hooked up in his region. Chang proved to be a alternatively anemic chief, however, and modified into not able to efficiently right the South Korean supply. His successors additionally had trouble, and with the useful resource of 1971, the then South Korean President Park Chung Hee felt the situation changed into awful enough to claim martial regulation. President Park then saved a great authoritarian grip at the nation for a good buy the rest of the remaining decade, until he modified into assassinated in October of 1979.

This darkish South Korean past seems so truly alien to the colorful and extraordinarily a fulfillment South Korea that we realize nowadays. Now, South Korea is idea no longer for martial law and civil unrest, but for being an economic and technological powerhouse. Today, South Korea is the land of Samsung telephones, Kia vehicles, LG

Electronics, and a significant experience of development. But it wasn't normally this way. In the aftermath of the Korean War and its next armistice, it did absolutely take the time for the Republic of Korea to get on its feet.

Chapter 11: Current Relations Between North

Few international locations in the international are as diametrically in opposition to every one-of-a-type as North and South Korea. But irrespective of the truth that ideology has pushed the ones factions aside, they're even though very hundreds merchandise of the equal subculture. And to make sure, there are Koreans on everything of the DMZ who lengthy for his or her u. S. To be reunited over again.

The first symptoms of a potential thawing of the icy courting amongst North and South Korea got here in 1998 beneath the control of South Korean President Kim Dai-jung, who carried out what he known as his "Sunshine Policy." The Sunshine Policy turn out to be a contemporary approach to inter-Korean people of the circle of relatives that pressured openness and talk.

At this issue, South Korea had extensively surpassed North Korea in financial achievement. North Korea, in the mean time, become funneling what meager resources it had into its military whilst the common North Korean confronted starvation. This bleak state of affairs furnished an possibility for the Sunshine Policy to be of use.

South Korea turn out to be to polish as a vibrant instance to the North Koreans suffering in the darkness of communist failure. But not excellent have become South Korea to be an example, it was to acquire out and lend a hand to help its faltering companion to the north. The openness of the Sunshine Policy brought on an open talk with the North that allowed for a so-called "summit" to take place in June of 2000, surely so the 2 aspects must openly talk with every one in all a kind.

This changed into quite a leap ahead, thinking about that there were no legit communicate some of the two warring factions for the cause that armistice had brought about a ceasefire in 1953. At this assembly, South Korean President Kim Dai-jung met with the successor of Kim Il-sung (who had considering handed), his son, Kim Jong-il. This have become then observed up thru every other in 2007 wherein Kim Jong-il stated the opportunity of "inter-Korean monetary cooperation responsibilities," with the then South Korean president, Roh Moo-hyun.

Kim Jong-il could likely pass away with out a excellent deal of a few factor coming of these overtures, but his son, Kim Jong-un, might preserve the way of existence of maintaining summits with South Korea in

2018, even as he met with South Korean President Moon Jae-in. Since then, North Korea had turn out to be a nuclear strength and had formerly threatened many elements of the arena with its nuclear saber-rattling. As such, the primary purpose of those 2018 talks have become each a de-escalation of those provocations and to get a pledge for an eventual denuclearization of the Korean Peninsula.

Initially, the summits seemed a success in this reason as they produced the so-known as "Panmunjom Declaration," wherein each elements agreed to "cooperate on formally finishing the Korean war" and the eventual denuclearization of the Korean Peninsula. It all sounded well and right, but on the stop of the day, it have come to be without a doubt communicate. Both aspects pledged to cooperate in seeking to officially cease the Korean War, but as of the time of writing, it's technically although ongoing. They additionally pledged to do away with nuclear guns, but the North remains production them.

Some have criticized such conferences as being nothing greater than propaganda victories for a duplicitous communist dictator who has no motive of creating well on any pledge of any kind. This truely might be actual. Kim Jong-un clearly is aware about that his nuclear arsenal is his quantity-one deterrent for regime alternate – so why might he need to ever supply them up?

But just because it seems not going that making headway with talks need to supply large alternate, that's no cause to no longer have them. Because if the arena had been to genuinely isolate and close to North Korea out once more, then all hope of a selection is misplaced.

It's particular to hold your pals close to however your enemies nearer, and South Korean leadership would probable concur with that sentiment. They might also as an alternative have a bit bit of dialogue open, to get a experience of what's occurring with North Korea, than to haven't any idea what is probably happening there.

Chapter 12: Japanese Control Of Korea

Koreans have been pressured to combat for Japan in World War Two

The Japanese Empire annexed Korea in 1910 and tried to break Korean manner of life within the years up to 1945.

The training machine forbade the talking of Korean in schools and universities as Japan tried to stress Koreans to speak Japanese. Thousands of books have been burned, and historical documents had been destroyed in an try and wipe out Korean subculture. Naturally, the Koreans fought all over again.

In this period, round 100,000 Japanese families settled in Korea, and approximately one million Koreans had been forced to move and artwork in Japan.

The Japanese destroyed many ancient homes, and people that had been not have been emerge as traveller points of hobby for wealthy Japanese net web page website online traffic.

World War Two and the defeat of Japan did now not suggest independence for Korea. Although Japanese rule modified into ended, the peninsula became divided alongside the 38th Parallel. This department was purported to be short-time period, however it have become eternal because of the Cold War maximum of the Soviet Union and the us.

A communist ruler subsidized thru the communist states of the Soviet Union and China have emerge as installation within the north. In the south, a capitalist government modified into supported by means of the usage of way of the usa and the newly common United Nations.

The Start of the Korean War

Thousands of South Koreans flee from the advancing North Korean Army

On August 15, 1948, South Korea (the Republic of Korea) have grow to be installation. Around one month later, the Democratic People's Republic of Korea (North Korea) became set up.

The border among North Korea and South Korea come to be artificial and had been drawn alongside the 38th Parallel. The North Korean chief, Kim Il-sung, desired to invade the south and make Korea one communist kingdom. In 1949, he requested the Soviet Union for help, but the Soviet chief, Joseph Stalin, refused.

Stalin didn't think that North Korea had the competencies to launch such an attack and become concerned about what the usa and its allies may additionally do.

Over the subsequent 3 hundred and sixty five days, the Korean chief built up the army right into a effective stress. When the Chinese despatched again many conflict-hardened Korean troops, and with Soviet tool, the North had turn out to be far more powerful than the south.

North Korean forces in 1950 numbered amongst a hundred and fifty,000 and two hundred,000. They were prepared into ten infantry divisions, a tank department, and a small air force. The North had two hundred fighter planes and three hundred tanks. The populace of North Korea modified into definitely over 9 million humans.

The populace of South Korea changed into 20 million. The South had around 98,000 troops, no tanks, and only a few fighter planes.

On June 25, 1950, at sunrise, North Korean troops crossed the thirty eighth Parallel with a large artillery bombardment as useful resource. By June 28, North Korean troops had taken the capital of the south, Seoul.

The United Nations jail army help for South Korea.

Timeline 2

On September 12, 1950, North Korean forces reached the 'Pusan Perimeter' of their beef up through South Korea.

The North Korean troops had been driven once more, and on September 25, 1950, the South Korean capital, Seoul, changed into liberated.

In October 1950, the North Korean Army end up pushed returned into North Korea. When the United Nations (UN) forces had been given near the Chinese border, Chinese troops entered North Korea and attacked. The UN forces retreated.

By December 1950, Chinese forces had succeeded in the usage of out American and UN forces from North Korea. However, the Chinese had misplaced many soldiers. It is expected that spherical eighty,000 have been killed or wounded.

The Pusan Perimeter

UN troops look ahead to some other assault thru the KPA

When the Korean People's Army (KPA) attacked Southern Korea, the United Nations despatched troops to help the South Korean forces, who had no longer been capable of prevent the attack.

By June 28, 1950, the KPA had taken the capital of South Korea, Seoul.

The US forces despatched to the Korean Peninsula couldn't halt the development of the KPA and had been pressured further and in addition another time.

South Korean, American, and British troops made a remaining stand in August in a protective area referred to as the Pusan Perimeter. This stretched for a hundred and forty miles at some point of the port of Busan.

What modified into to spread amongst August four and September 18, 1950, become the number one maximum critical struggle of the Korean War.

The South Korean, American, and British forces numbered one hundred forty,000.

The North Korean strain (KPA) numbered 98,000.

After being continuously defeated by way of the usage of the KPA, the combat round Busan could be critical.

The UN forces fought off repeated attacks for six weeks. The air superiority of the UN forces supposed that the KPA had large problems with supply traces.

A landing in the again of the KPA troops at Inchon introduced approximately the fall apart of the North Korean resistance, and that they retreated to the border.

UN Forces Attack North Korea

US tank crew take a ruin

With the South Korean capital, Seoul, lower again inside the arms of the South Koreans and the North Koreans on their thing of the border, it modified into choice time.

The idea to invade the north was legal, and on October 7, 1950, UN troops crossed the border.

On October 12, UN Forces captured the North Korean capital, Pyongyang, and moved toward the border with communist China. The state of affairs had been reversed.

China acted rapid and despatched 250,000 troops to assist combat the UN Forces.

The ferocity of the attack with the useful resource of Chinese troops crushed the UN troops, and that they were forced decrease again over the border after suffering heavy losses.

Timeline 3

On January four, 1951, North Korean and Chinese troops recaptured Seoul.

On March 14, 1951, UN forces liberated Seoul from communist troops.

In April 1951, the American President, Harry S. Truman, relieved General MacArthur of the command in Korea. He positioned General Mathew Ridgeway in command.

Peace talks started out out on July 10, 1951, but the preventing persevered.

The Chinese Attack South Korea

Fighting in the streets of Seoul

With the fulfillment of using the United Nations troops out of North Korea, The Chinese chief, Mao Zedong, perception it have become possible to take South Korea and unify the Korean peninsula.

The begin of the Chinese offensive in January 1951 resulted within the Chinese taking the South Korean capital, Seoul. The Chinese noticed that the resistance of the South Korean troops become the vulnerable link within the United Nations Army, and that they exploited it completely.

For the Americans, the improvement of Chinese forces into South Korea was considered a catastrophe. The American navy commander General MacArthur stated that he concept the only way in advance turn out to be to defeat the Chinese with the beneficial useful resource of the use of America's nuclear weapons. The American President did now not echo this opinion. However, the exhausted Chinese and North Korean forces ran out of steam and were in the end held with the useful resource of the UN forces. This revived the morale of UN troops.

In March 1951, there was a counteroffensive towards the Chinese. This led to the recapture of Seoul, which were devastated with the useful resource of the normal attacks from each facets.

Over a million human beings had populated the capital town of South Korea earlier than the struggle, but in March 1951, this populace had faded to plenty less than two hundred,000. There modified right into a loss of sanitation, scientific additives, and meals and water. Many human beings were ravenous.

In the spring of 1951, the UN forces superior a few miles into North Korea and organized defensive lines as a buffer to prevent the Chinese from reinvading. This modified into finished to stop Seoul from falling into enemy hands yet again.

In April 1951, a Chinese counter-assault aimed to interrupt thru the buffer vicinity and retake Seoul. The events across the Imjin River observed the Chinese decorate held up by manner of the British. The British were outnumbered with the aid of the Chinese however hung on for 3 days earlier than being forced to retreat.

The struggle of Imjin River was one of the deadliest fought in the course of the Korean War. The end result enabled UN forces to withdraw to a more potent protecting function near Seoul, wherein the Chinese broaden become ultimately halted.

The preventing across the Imjin River modified into the remaining fantastic conflict of the 'cellular phase' of the warfare in Korea. Both sides discovered out that an entire victory may be nearly not viable to achieve.

Negotiations for a truce were commenced in July 1951 at Kaesong, but a deal emerge as not reached until 1953.

While the negotiating groups from the two aspects argued, the troops from each additives fought skirmishes to advantage control of strategic areas. The preventing changed into carried out each in severe cold or blistering warm temperature. The idea behind most army operations from 1951 onwards modified into to beautify the negotiating feature for the upcoming truce.

Chapter 13: General Douglas Macarthur

General MacArthur observes the troops landing at Inchon

When the communist troops from North Korea invaded South Korea in June 1950, Douglas MacArthur changed into given command of america-led coalition of UN troops.

Under his command, the North Koreans were pressured once more over the border and then were pushed returned to the Chinese border.

When the Chinese retaliated, MacArthur favored using nuclear bombs towards them. The American President, Harry S. Truman, turned into worried that an attack might start World War Three and that the Soviet Union may get involved. Because of this, he refused to authorize an attack on the Chinese mainland.

President Truman found out in April 1951 that MacArthur changed into completely inside the lower back of escalating the battle in Korea in place of restricting it. He removed the general from command.

MacArthur once more to the united states in April 1951 and became welcomed again as a conflict hero. He publically criticized the suggestions of the president.

There have been calls for him to run for president because the Republican candidate, but Dwight Eisenhower modified into selected.

MacArthur died in 1964, aged 84.

The First Battle of Seoul

North Korean leader Kim Il-sung ordered the attack at the south

The war passed off among June 25 and June 28, 1950.

The North Korean forces crossed the 38th Parallel on June 25, 1950. There were troops supported with the resource of artillery and tanks.

The South Korean Army couldn't deal with the velocity and ferocity of the assault. They had no tanks and no anti-tank guns.

The South Korean forces retreated, and the North Korean Army occupied Seoul on the 28th of June.

As a cease result of the assault, the President of america, Harry S. Truman, promised to assist, and the United Nations Security Council (UNSC) surpassed Resolution 80 4. This choice criminal assist to South Korea.

South Korea had 65,000 troops

North Korea had 107, 0000 troops

South Korean losses blanketed forty four,000 missing, wounded, or vain.

North Korean losses have been 1,112 Injured or useless

An emphatic victory for North Korea.

The Battle of Osan

The arrival of Task Force Smith in South Korea

The Battle of Osan occurred on July 5, 1950, at Osan in South Korea.

This emerge as the number one time that American troops had arise in competition to North Korean forces in the warfare.

An American task pressure named Task Force Smith arrived at Osan near Seoul, with orders to postpone the North Korean increase until greater US troops should arrive. The American undertaking force lacked the anti-tank system had to save you the North Koreans. The North Korean tanks swept via Task Force Smith and persisted to enhance.

The Americans then engaged with spherical five,000 North Korean troops and had been ultimately crushed.

The American assignment pressure retreated, having failed in its project.

The US forces numbered 540 troops

The North Koreans had 36 tanks and five,000 infantry

There were 60 Americans killed, 21 wounded, and eighty two captured.

There were forty two North Koreans killed, 80 5 wounded, and one tank destroyed

This changed right into a victory for North Korea

The Battle of Inchon (Incheon)

USS Toledo shells the shoreline in advance than the troops land

The Battle of Inchon passed off among September 10 and September 15, 1950.

The warfare involved a UN pressure of troops and 261 naval ships.

The war started out out on September 15 with the landing of UN troops from ships onto the beaches close to the town of Incheon. There changed into a heavy naval bombardment that supported the touchdown.

This have become a risky and daredevil assault masterminded by using way of the use of the American General, Douglas MacArthur.

The assault coincided with the breakout of UN forces from the Pusan Perimeter. The North Korean troops retreated with heavy losses.

Troops from the united states, UK, and Canada numbered forty,000

Soldiers from North Korea numbered 6,500

The UN out of place 209 troops with 809 wounded

350 North Korean troops were killed

This come to be a victory for the United Nations and the South Koreans.

The Second Battle of Seoul

UN troops take lower once more Seoul avenue thru avenue

The Second Battle of Seoul happened in overdue September 1950 and resulted within the UN forces retaking the capital of South Korea.

After the UN troop landings at Inchon and the breakout of the Pusan Perimeter, the charge of the improvement closer to communist-held Seoul changed into gradual.

The stopping modified into fierce, especially due to the advent of two crack-preventing gadgets from the Korean People's Army (KPA). The KPA desired to stall the UN offensive to allow Seoul to be bolstered and moreover for the withdrawal of troops from the south.

The retaking of the capital have come to be important to General MacArthur, despite the truth that he knew that concentrating on the metropolis may also permit lots of North Korean troops to break out back to North Korea.

As UN troops entered Seoul, they were faced with formidable resistance. The North Koreans had constructed their defense positions properly within the town, and at instances, the preventing modified into from residence to house.

Anxious to inform the sector that Seoul had fallen, it end up introduced that Seoul have been liberated at 2 pm on September 25. In truth, it would take an additional days for the combating to prevent.

The UN forces consisted of 40,000 troops from america, South Korea, the United Kingdom, and Canada.

The North Korean troops numbered 7,000.

About 4 hundred UN troops have been killed

Several thousand North Korean troops had been both killed, wounded, or taken prisoner.

The war became a victory for the UN.

The Battle of Ch'ongch'on River

This war took place among November 25 and December 2, 1950.

The Chinese had entered the conflict whilst UN troops have been given too near the China, North Korean border. They had succeeded in forcing the UN troops lower again within the route of South Korea. As a freezing wintry weather closed in and the snow fell closely, the Chinese attacked UN positions at Ch'ongch'on River.

The Chinese Army attacked UN forces in the Ch'ongch'on River valley on the night time time of November 25, 1950. Although the UN forces averted being surrounded thru the Chinese, they suffered heavy casualties and have been forced to retreat.

The war led to all UN forces withdrawing to the 38th Parallel.

The UN had 250,000 troops from america, South Korea, Turkey, and the United Kingdom.

The Chinese and North Korean troops numbered 230,000.

Around 11,000 UN troops had been killed, wounded, or lacking.

The Chinese and North Koreans had 10,000 warfare casualties.

This changed proper right into a decisive victory for China, which freed North Korea from UN forces.

The Battle of Chosin Reservoir

UN troops ruin thru the Chinese strains

This war came about round four weeks after the Chinese had entered the battle. China's chief, Mao Zedong, had ordered his navy commanders to interrupt the United Nations forces. The stopping became fierce amongst November 27 and December 13,

1950. The snow made conditions pretty tough.

The UN forces were taken completely via wonder via the Chinese assault. What accompanied for the following 17 days grow to be a brutal war in freezing situations.

Around 30,000 UN troops have been surrounded and attacked thru a hundred twenty,000 Chinese troops. Even even though the UN troops had been outnumbered, they had been able to break through and retreat to the port of Hungnam. They inflicted heavy casualties at the Chinese troops.

The retreat of the UN troops after the Battle of Ch'ongch'on River and the evacuation from the port of Hungnam marked the entire withdrawal of UN troops from North Korea.

The UN pressure consisted of 30,000 US, UK, and South Korean troops, of which spherical

13,000 have been killed, wounded, or lacking.

There were an predicted a hundred twenty,000 Chinese troops, of which an anticipated 60,000 were killed or wounded.

Chapter 14: The Third Battle Of Seoul

This struggle is likewise known as the Chinese New Year Offensive, and it got here after the Chinese defeated UN forces on the Battle of Ch'ongch'on River.

After this defeat through the Chinese, the UN forces were at an rock backside, and it became pondered leaving the Korean Peninsula.

On the orders of Chinese chief Mao Zedong, the Chinese Army crossed the 38th Parallel and headed for Seoul. This have become an try to stress all distant places troops out of South Korea.

With the improvement of Chinese troops, Seoul turned into evacuated on January three, 1951.

The Chinese Army captured Seoul, however the assault had the opportunity effect to what Mao Zedong had supposed. Instead of demoralizing, the UN forces it stirred up aid to shield South Korea.

The UN Army might also want to soon go on the offensive, and the Chinese troops were exhausted after having fought their manner into the capital.

The UN pressure numbered round 136,000 and changed into crafted from infantrymen from the us, South Korea, the United Kingdom, Thailand, and Australia. There have been about 800 casualties and deaths.

The Chinese Army had 170,000 infantrymen. There had been around 8,000 each killed or wounded.

Even no matter the truth that this end up each other victory for China and North Korea, tactically, it emerge as a defeat as it reignited the United Nations into taking lower back South Korea.

Operation Ripper

UN air superiority executed a large element within the Korean War

Operation Ripper is often called the fourth Battle of Seoul. It took place among March 7 and April 4, 1951.

Operation Ripper end up designed to damage as heaps of the Chinese Army as viable and retake Seoul and the 38th Parallel. Before the assault started out out, UN artillery bombarded the Chinese within the most important artillery bombardment of the Korean War.

www.ingramcontent.com/pod-product-compliance
Lightning Source LLC
Chambersburg PA
CBHW071443080526
44587CB00014B/1972